Immigrant Parents'
Involvement In Schools:

A Case Study of Somali Parents

Abdullahi M. Ahmed, Ed.D.

Immigrant Parents' Involvement In Schools:

A Case Study of Somali Parents

Abdullahi M. Ahmed, Ed.D.

The University of Maine
DigitalCommons@UMaine

ACKNOWLEDGEMENTS

First and foremost, I thank the greatest teacher in my life, my mother. She did not have formal education, yet she taught me the value of education and the importance of hard work. Thank you for selling vegetables in the streets of Mogadishu in order to support me and my siblings.

Aside from my mother, I would like to thank my advisor and chair of my dissertation committee, Sarah (Sally) Mackenzie, for her patience, guidance, and for mentoring me through my doctoral work. She believed in me and pushed me to my limits as only a caring and knowledgeable teacher and mentor can do. I am eternally grateful to you and thank you for all the contributions to my journey.

I am also very grateful for the support and generosity of the time and expertise of Gordon Donaldson and Flynn Ross. I thank you, Gordon, for believing in me and allowing me to become part of the doctoral cohort. I remember you commuted several times from Ellsworth, Maine to my workplace in Portland to give me feedback. Thank you for accommodating my work schedule. Thank you, Flynn, for joining my committee and staying with me in this long journey. You are a gifted teacher and scholar, and of course, my role model.

Finding an outside committee members was not an easy task for me. I thank Julie Canniff of the University of Southern Maine and John Maddaus of University of Maine for joining my committee. Thank you, Julie, for reading and editing multiple drafts of my dissertation. Thank you, John, for your feedback. Listening to you makes me think of how important it is to pay attention to details. I am grateful for your support.

Aside from my committee members, I thank my wife, Zamzam, for her support. I cannot imagine what this doctoral process would have been like without the support of Zamzam. I also want to thank my children, Bilan, Balqies, Bilal, and Safa for being so patient with me. They skipped many play days with their friends because I was studying at the library.

ISBN-13: 9781544119267

ISBN-10: 1544119267

Recommended Citation

Ahmed, Abdullahi, "Somali Parents' Involvement in the
Education of Their Children in American Middle Schools:
a Case Study in Portland, Maine" (2015). *Electronic Theses
and Dissertations*. 2402.

http://digitalcommons.library.umaine.edu/etd/2402

TABLE OF CONTENTS

CHAPTER ONE: INTRODUCTION..................................1

CHAPTER TWO: LITERATURE REVIEW...................19

CHAPTER THREE: METHODOLOGY..............................59

CHAPTER FOUR: PRESENTATION OF THE DATA...83

CHAPTER FIVE: ANALYSIS...............................143

CHAPTER SIX: DISCUSSION OF THE FINDINGS AND IMPLICATIONS..181

REFERENCES..211

BIOGRAPHY OF THE AUTHOR.......................225

DISSERTATION SUBMISSIONS.......................229

CHAPTER ONE
INTRODUCTION

Problem

Members of language minority groups are not a monolithic group although they share some similarities. Different subgroups have their unique characteristics, yet the U.S. education system treats all immigrants and English Language Learners (ELL) as somewhat the same. Generally, ELL students are treated in a "one size fits all" model. This approach is, perhaps, understandable because of the tremendous influx of immigrants and the internal and external challenges that schools face, including political, financial, legal, and ethical ones. However, this approach flies in the face of the notion of cultural competency as a caring and just way to treat all children in school (Barrera, 2006; Hosp & Reschly, 2004).

Cultural competence refers to

> having an awareness of one's own cultural identity and views about difference, and the ability to learn and build on the varying cultural and community norms of students and their families. It is the ability to understand the within-group differences that make each student unique, while celebrating the between-

1

group variations that make our country a tapestry. This understanding informs and expands teaching practices in the culturally competent educator's classroom (National Education Association, 2013).

It is a two-way street: Newcomers need to learn about the culture and norms of their new home; yet educators, to be effective and equitable, need to learn about the culture, values, and understandings of their students, no matter where they are from. One of the major differences educators would come to understand has to do with the ways in which other ethnic and cultural groups view education and interact with the institution of schooling. A lack of understanding on both sides can create major challenges for educators and newcomers alike.

For example, some recent research on Latino families indicates that language minority parents and their children's teachers have different perceptions and expectations of education and the role of parents in their children's schooling. There is a clear indication that Latino parents' perceptions and expectations are not aligned with the ways American schools function (Crespo-Jimenez, 2010). Research shows that the single largest barrier to language minority parental involvement in public education is unfamiliarity of the parents with complex processes of U.S.

public education (Scribner, 1999). Ironically, immigrant parents are often blamed for their lack of involvement in the education of their children even though schools and educators have not investigated the cultural, economic, behavioral, and ethnographic factors which influence parental views on education and schooling and their involvement in the schools of their children (Zentella, 2002).

One place that has repeatedly experienced the challenges related to the needs of immigrant populations is Portland, Maine. Portland is the largest city in Maine, with nearly 67,000 residents, fifteen percent of who are from minority groups. Portland Public Schools serve about 7000 students. The city has 10 elementary schools, three middle schools, four high schools, and one adult school. The school system is diverse. About 30% of the students are from language minority families representing more than 55 languages.

Somali students and their parents in Portland are among the most recent newcomer refugee populations. The majority of Somalis in the U.S. came to the country as refugees after 1988. Just like any ethnic and social group, Somali refugees in the U.S. have unique characteristics (Arman & Kapteijins, 2004), and Somali group identity has sparked controversies in many communities. Nationwide, language minority students' academic achievement as a group has raised concerns for educators.

Somalis make up more than ten percent of the student population of the Portland schools. As much as educators wish and try to integrate these students into American schools, they have fallen short. Administrators, teachers, and support personnel do what they can, but they know little about the culture or the people. And there has been almost no research or information to guide them, especially pertaining to Somali people's understanding and perceptions of education in general and about schooling in the United States in particular. This newcomer group represents the tensions of cultural competence as educators seek to engage parents effectively in their children's school experience. If there is to be culturally competent teaching and integration of Somali parents and students into schools, educators need to know more about the culture and, specifically, the views of Somali parents regarding education and schooling.

Having presented the problem of the study, the rest of the chapter provides background for the study. It is followed by a description of the specific context of the study, Portland, Maine, then the purpose and the significance of this research.

Background

The following paragraphs provide background to the
problem by describing the increasing numbers and needs of
immigrant students to the US, the importance of parental
involvement to children's academic achievement, and the
promise of culturally competent teaching and learning for all
children in the country, especially English Language
Learners. It ends with a brief description of the Theory of
Planned Behavior that describes the factors that affect
behavior in individuals and underpins the study of immigrant
parent involvement.

Minority Students' Achievement and Parental Involvement

Research shows that the school dropout rate is highest
in high-poverty communities, where the student body is
predominantly Black and Latino (Orfield, Losen, Wald, &
Swanson, 2004). The academic success and frequent failure
of low-income and language minority students has received
the significant attention of stakeholders at all levels. Reform
initiatives were designed to close the achievement gap
between minority students and their peers and sometimes
address the opportunity gap (Ladson-Billings, 2006).
Congress passed laws such as the No Child Left Behind Act
of 2001, and states and municipalities devised their own

5

policies and initiatives to mitigate the issue (Rodriguez, 2012). As a natural outcome, the attention and the widespread mobilization around low academic performance and the high dropout rate of minority students, in addition to issues of some students' socially deviant behaviors, has resulted in greater accountability and more test-centered practices. Yet, studies show that minority students continue to perform below the levels of achievement of their white, middle class peers.

Laws such as the No Child Left Behind Act of 2001 aspire to create opportunities for parents to have influence on their children's education (Crespo-Jimenez 2010; GOALS 2000: Educate America Act, 1994; NCLB Act, 2001). According to the spirit of the law, the aim of the educators and institutions must be to provide opportunities for all students and requires that local authorities devise policy compacts developed with and approved by parents. Schools must not neglect the educational needs of any group of students representing any degree of ability nor their families, including language minorities. Moreover, ignoring the requirements of the state and federal laws can place school systems in financial risk. In order to address the mandates and students' needs, educators expect support from parents but are not sure how to engage them.

According to federal law, school districts must meaningfully involve all parents in the processes of their children's education (NCLB Act, 2001). Parental involvement can boost student achievement and the chances of student graduation (Baker & Soden, 1998; Peterson, 1999). Underachievement of Hispanic students, the largest language minority group in the U.S., is correlated with the lack of parental involvement of the group (Crespo-Jimenez, 2010; Scribner, 1999). However, contrary to what many educators believe about Latino parental involvement, Crespo-Jimenez (2010), found that Latino parents care about their children's education, but they want schools to lead by reducing barriers that limit parental involvement (Christenson & Sheridan, 2001). Latino parents believe that they are involved in their children's education and are willing to increase their involvement, yet they need help in becoming more involved (Crespo-Jimenez, 2010).

Cultural Competence

People from different cultural and religious groups live together as one community in many cities in the U.S. In multicultural societies, individual cultural groups maintain their identities and their culture. However, there are mainstream norms and cultural characteristics that constitute the dominant culture. Communities of certain cultural backgrounds (minorities) have to function in two different and sometimes contradictory ways (Banks & Banks, 2003).

Students, regardless of their social class, race, immigration status, or other cultural characteristics, are guaranteed equal opportunity to learn. However, it is understandable that some students, because of their cultural characteristics have a better chance than others who do not belong to the dominant culture. The effects of sociocultural barriers in the education of the minority students are identified and documented. Students from lower socioeconomic families generally perform lower in schools (Ogbu, 1978). Efforts have been made to mitigate the effects of these barriers. To work toward the elimination of minority students' underachievement, it is necessary to employ culturally competent pedagogy and interventions.

Demographic shifts in the U.S. are becoming significant, and groups of students once considered as minorities are becoming the majority in some school districts. As a result, public schools have begun to emphasize cultural competence. Teacher preparation programs have redesigned their courses to incorporate cultural competence knowledge and added courses to meet ELL teaching endorsement requirements. Schools have allocated time for professional development; they have recruited minority educators, and

8

established centers for interpretation and translation such as the Multilingual Office of Portland Public Schools in Maine.

In Portland, Maine, the demographic changes in the United States, with an increasing number of language minority students, magnifies the importance of addressing the needs of minority students and their families. The Multilingual Office was founded in 1980 with grant monies to support children, families, and teachers in promoting access to quality schooling. Currently, the Multilingual Office of Portland Public Schools serves language minority families by enrolling their children in the schools and assisting with translating and interpreting documents. It also provides professional development for staff as well as employing multicultural community and family specialists who mediate between the cultural communities and the school communities to help students become multicultural.

English Language Learners in the United States

Language minority students comprise one of the largest minority groups in U.S. public schools. According to Park (2007), in the U.S. the number of English Language Learners, or school-age children whose first language is not English, and who are in the process of learning English, jumped from 3.1 million to 5.1 million in ten years between 1995 to 2005. The population of immigrants as a percentage of the total population in the U.S. has increased from 4.7% in 1970 to 12.9% in 2010 (U.S. Census, 2010). In the year 2000 the number of immigrants reached 28.4 million, and they accounted for one in every ten Americans. In 2010 the number jumped to 39.9 million, which is about twelve percent of the total U.S. population (U.S. Census, 2010).

The rapid increase of the ELL population in the last four decades is due to immigration patterns and is even more dramatic in the school-age population. According to the U.S. Department of Education, the number of ELL students enrolled in public schools increased 160% between the 1989-1990 school year and the 2004-2005 school year as compared to an increase of only 20% of the total school age enrollment (National Center for Education Statistics, 2014). Despite the increasing number of ELL students in North America, Artiles and Klingner (2007) and Haager (2007) admit that little is known about the ELL subgroups as students other than the fact that they do not perform as well as their American-born peers on standardized assessments and that their achievements are below grade level expectations. ELL students as a group are by definition globally diverse, so their characteristics as learners vary widely with many nuanced differences.

Theory of Reasoned Action and Theory of Planned Behavior

The theoretical framework for this study is found in the intersection of perception and behavior. The Theory of Reasoned Action (TRA) and its enhanced version, the Theory of Planned Behavior (TPB), are the most suitable theories to situate this work. These theories were used previously as frameworks for a similar study in which the patterns of Latino parental involvement were explored (Crespo-Jimenez, 2010).

The Theory of Planned Behavior consists of several elements. Behavioral intention indicates a person's relative beliefs and attitude to perform (or not to perform) a behavior. In other words, behavior is influenced by an individual's perceptions and beliefs about the consequences of performing the behavior and by his or her evaluation of these consequences (Ajzen, 1991). The framework demonstrates that parents' decisions to become involved (or not) in the schools of their school age children can be influenced by a number of factors including parents' perceptions about education, parenting, public schools, teaching and teachers, and child development. Normative beliefs or subjective norms are the second element of TPB. It is seen as a combination of perceived expectations from relevant

11

individuals or groups along with an individual's intention to comply with these expectations. In other words, parents' perceptions of and beliefs about the people who are important to them and what behaviors are socially accepted by those important people influence their behaviors (Ajzen & Fishbein, 1980). To put the first two elements of the theory into simple terms: a person's voluntary behavior is predicted by her beliefs about that behavior and how she thinks other people would view her if she performed the behavior. The third element of TPB refers to the perceived control beliefs. It is a person's perception of ease or difficulty to perform a behavior and is called "perceived control beliefs." A person's beliefs, combined with subjective norms and her beliefs about the presence of barriers and opportunities for performing a behavior form her behavioral intention and behavior.

The significance of using TPB for the discussion of this study is relevant because it relates an individual's intention to perform a behavior, not only to her beliefs about the behavior and behavioral norms (what other people think about the behavior) but also to the amount of control the individual possesses. In other words, both what they perceive of the behavior and environmental factors are used to predict intentions and behavior. That is why TPB is suitable for a study in which the goal is to explore participants' perceptions about parental involvement in education and schools and what other factors (other than their perceptions) influence parents' decisions to be involved or not involved. Inability to understand English, unfamiliarity with the U.S. education system, and cultural factors can limit parental involvement of language minority groups (Arias & Morillo-Campbell, 2008). For example, a parent may perceive that she is involved even if it is not in the way a school might expect, or a person might perceive that involvement is a desirable thing but does not have the ability or the knowledge of what or how to be involved.

Context of the Study

The research site of this study is Portland, Maine. Portland is a coastal city in Maine, one of the six New England states with an estimated population of 66,200. It is the most diverse and populated city in the entire state of Maine. About 15% of the total population is from minority groups. Although the city has lower than average median household income, it has a high percentage of college graduates. According to the Maine Department of Education, Portland Public Schools have close to an 80% average graduation rate. The diversity in the student body and their families poses instructional, organizational, and economic challenges to the school system.

Purpose of the Study

The purpose of the case study was to explore perceptions of the parents of Somali children who are in Portland Public Schools regarding education and schooling of their children and the perceptions and behavior of these parents regarding their involvement in their children's education and schooling. For the purpose of this study, *parental involvement* was defined as parental work with children in education and in schools and with educators to make sure their children succeed. The term *education* was defined as the act of preparing children intellectually for a productive life. It encompasses many aspects of the educative process of children including public and religious schooling, while *schooling* is defined as institutionalization of education in grades and with a curriculum. The investigation builds on Crespo-Jimenez's (2010) study, which examined the patterns of involvement of Latino parents with middle school children in the education process. The exploration was accomplished through surveys and personal interviews with Somali parents.

Significance

Conducting research in this area of newcomers and their views on education and schooling is a complex undertaking. Understanding the factors influencing Somali refugee parental involvement in the schools of their children requires sorting through the issues that may be unique to Somali refugee parents such as culture and their understanding of the English language. Literature suggests that parental involvement is affected by the interplay of the refugee cultures and mainstream American culture. Balancing work and school involvement is another example of challenges parents face (Crespo-Jimenez, 2010). In an effort to learn directly from Somali parents, the study described here attempts to identify the views of Somali refugee parents on education and schooling and how these views influence their intentions and behavior regarding their involvement in their children's education and schools.

Capturing the views of Somali parents concerning education in general and schooling and parental involvement in particular can have practical implications for educators and policy makers. The findings from the study contribute to the existing knowledge about language minority parents and their involvement in their children's educations in general, and Somali parents' views and perceptions in particular. The study contributes to the efforts of scholars and practitioners in finding better ways to meet the needs of language minority students and their parents and will aid educators and school leaders in educating students whose needs have not been met in the education system as it presently exists. The findings from the study question the common approach of viewing all language minority children as monolithic and emphasize the importance of understanding other cultures as educators seek to become culturally competent. Additionally, it is the first ethnographic study of Somali refugee parents using the Theory of Planned Behavior.

In short, in Portland, and other cities with similar refugee populations, educators' understanding of Somali parents' perceptions, and intentions and behavior regarding their involvement in their children's education can enhance the process of creating culturally competent and responsive program interventions, which, in turn, can contribute to mitigating the challenges Somali students and other immigrants and refugees face in adjusting to and learning in American schools.

The next chapter begins with an overview of the characteristics of newcomers in the United States in general and a closer look at Somalis specifically, followed by brief discussion of the legal mandates of English Language

Learners education in the U.S. The remaining sections will address parental involvement and the factors that influence language minority parents' perceptions of and involvement in the education and schooling of their children. It concludes with the conceptual framework that guides the design of the study.

CHAPTER TWO
LITERATURE REVIEW

The study explores the views of a refugee population of parents on education and schooling, and their views about their involvement in their children's education. There are four major areas that need to be discussed in order for the reader to understand the grounding of this study. The first area has to do with a discussion of the Somali refugees themselves, their history, culture, and experiences of schooling. The second area involves a discussion of the policies and their implementation that relate to the education of English Language Learners (ELL) in the United States. Thirdly, it is important for the reader to be acquainted with the literature on parental involvement in schools, generally, and specifically, as related to parents of ELL students. ELL students do graduate from separate classes for language learners to regular classes. In fact, parents often prefer that their children quickly move from the sheltered environment of such classes in order to assimilate more quickly into classes with a mix of all students. Nevertheless, the research has primarily focused on students and parents who are labeled as ELL, but the immigrant students and parents who may no longer be ELL share the same perceptions and have the same background experiences that apply to those in ELL classes.

Finally, the chapter provides an explanation of the theory that is used to frame the design of the study. The use of social science theories might be limited in this chapter because most qualitative case studies, traditionally, focus on the description of the case and not on theory (Creswell, 2007). The chapter ends with the conceptual framework of the study. The conceptual framework will guide the implementation of the study.

The term "immigrant" is loosely used to describe all language minority communities as well as language majority newcomers from other countries. Legally, however, language minorities can be grouped by the reasons they came to the United States. The first language minority group is immigrants. Immigrants have come to the U.S willingly and had the option to stay in their countries of origin. They embrace and learn the American way of life and assimilate in their new communities more quickly. Early in the twentieth century, most immigrants to the U.S. came from Western Europe and Canada. Job opportunities and social relations were often the reasons for their relocation (Berry, Boski, & Kim, 1988; Garcia, 1994).

Sojourners are the people who come to the United States to stay in the country for a limited time and return to their countries. They come to the U.S. willingly, mainly, for education and training or temporary employment. Unlike immigrants and refugees, they know that their stay is limited and do not need to learn the U.S. culture. Students from wealthy Gulf nations such as Saudi Arabia who are studying in American universities are examples of sojourners. Migrant workers from Central America are in a category close to sojourners because their stay in the U.S. is limited although their economic status is significantly different from sojourners who come to study.

Refugees are different from both immigrants and sojourners. They came to the United States because they were forced to leave their homeland. Many of them have left their family members in their original countries or in refugee camps. Many refugees have experienced physical and emotional trauma before coming to the U.S. Refugees, often, tend not to assimilate as quickly and maintain their culture in the new location (Berry, Boski, & Kim, 1988). They hope that their stay is limited and that one day they will have the opportunity to return to their home. In the U.S. refugees move together to single geographical locations. Somalis, who are refugees, have settled in large communities: Minneapolis and St. Paul, Minnesota, Columbus, Ohio, Seattle, Washington, and Portland and Lewiston, Maine.

Somali Culture, History, and Education

Somalia is located in the eastern-most part of the Horn of Africa: Kenya to the south, Ethiopia to the west, the Gulf of Aden to the north, and the Indian Ocean to the east border it. Topographically, there are plains in the south, mountains in the north, and deserts in the middle and the west. The land of Somalia is about 637,657 square miles with an estimated population of 10,085,638. The country has the longest coast of mainland of Africa, yet it is considered one of the poorest nations in the world with a high infant mortality rate, and a short life expectancy of 43 years (United Nations Educational Scientific and Cultural Organization [UNESCO], 1985). Somalia has a hot climate with an irregular rainfall.

Culture of Somalia

According to UNESCO (1985) more than 65% of Somalis are nomads. Somali people speak the Somali language, and because of their religious affiliation and geographical proximity, Somalis have strong connections to the Middle East and other parts of Asia. These connections elevated Arabic as one of the preferred and official languages of the country (Abdikadir & Cassanelli, 2007). Italian and

English are also spoken in Somalia (UNESCO, 1985). Despite the high illiteracy rate, Somalis have strong oral traditions and memorization abilities. Poetry, songs, rituals, and stories are passed to younger generation orally (Farid & McMahan, 2004). Overall the literacy rate has been, and is currently, very low in part due to the non-existing or limited infrastructure to support government schools, tradition, lack of stability, and conflicts. Furthermore, Somali was not a written language until the 1970s.

History of Somalia

Somalia had special importance for the ancient world. Somalis controlled parts of the Indian Ocean and the Red Sea and dominated the regional trade. Archeological facts connect Somalia to merchants from ancient Egypt (Farid & McMahan, 2004). Islamic education was the only educational system available to Somalis before the invasion of Somalia by the European colonial powers (Italy, Great Britain, and France) in the late nineteenth century and its subsequent division into five territories. Earlier, the local rulers in the main cities, like Mogadishu, were loosely affiliated with the Othman Caliphates or other Muslim rulers (Abdikadir & Cassanelli, 2007).

During the colonial period, Somalis resisted the European invaders militarily. They also opposed the

23

missionary and the colonial authorities' education models. The British and the Italians failed or perhaps did not want to educate large numbers of Somalis. The colonizers were, however, able to recruit and educate a small portion of the population, many of whom became military personnel and the employees of the colonial authorities (Abdikadir & Cassanelli, 2007).

Southern and Northern Somalia gained independence simultaneously from Italy and Great Britain in 1960. The people elected their first parliament and president. The government system remained democratic, and elections were held every four years. In 1969, after eight years under a democratic system, the president was assassinated and the military, led by General Mohamed Siyad Barre, executed a bloodless coup. General Barre ruled the country with an iron fist for 21 years. Since the fall of General Barre's regime in 1991, there has been no effective central government in Somalia. The civil war that started in 1991 continues today. Currently, there is a very weak government, which is unable to control most of the country. Islamic extremists affiliated with Al-Qaida control parts of Southern Somalia. Local semi-autonomous governments control the rest. Hundreds of thousands of Somalis have lost their lives, and millions have left the country. Close to one million Somalis live in refugee camps in neighboring Kenya and Ethiopia. In addition, many Somalis live in many if not all-major Western cities. It is estimated that close to a half million Somalis live in North America alone.

Education in Somalia

As a result of Somalia's turbulent history, the education system is complicated and has been fractured by conflicts of various kinds. However, there are some distinct historical milestone events that have contributed to the history of Somali education. Islamic teachings, Somali culture, and the colonization of Somalia by European powers are the major contributors.

History of the Somali Education System. The Somali system of education and other government institutions were formed after independence from the Britain and Italy was achieved in 1960. French Somaliland remained under the rule of France until the late 1970s, and later became an independent nation, Djibouti. Northern and Southern Somalia united days after they obtained their independence from the British and the Italian authorities respectively. For the first time Somalis were able to determine their own affairs. Like any other infant nation, selecting an official language for the country was a challenging task (Wei, 2000). Powerful elites who were educated in either Italian or English inherited the leadership of the country from their colonial masters. Meanwhile, religious groups pushed for the adaptation of Arabic, and nationalist movements favored the ethnic language, Somali (Farid & McMahan, 2004).

After the collapse of General Mohamed Siyad Barre's regime in 1991, there was no effective Somali government in place. The education background discussed here is the system that existed before 1991. Since 1991, different local and international non-governmental organizations have run the educational system in Somalia. Different curriculum materials are used by different organizations. Almost no schools use the old centralized Somali curriculum, which was used before the civil war started. According to Abdikadir and Cassanelli (2007), in the mid-1960s the Somali government was able to come up with one centralized educational system in which Arabic and English became the languages of instruction for elementary and secondary education respectively. Assigning or using different languages for different roles and circumstances was not unique to Somalis. It is a common practice in multilingual societies and in colonized countries (Wei, 2000).

It was only during the early 1970s when the ruling military general decided to make the Somali language the official language of the nation. Somalis of all walks of life

give the socialist ruler, Mohamed Siyad Barre, credit for
creating the script form of the Somali language. Barre is
credited with writing the Somali language and printing a
national curriculum for the government schools in a relatively
short time. The military regime built new schools, and many
children were able to go to school. For the first time in
Somali history, attending primary school for young children
in the major cities became an expectation in the 1970s.
Although some Somalis cautioned that adoption of the
Somali language could hinder nation building efforts and
would place Somalis who graduate from Somali schools at a
disadvantage in the global market, critics could not deny the
advantage of using the local language in instruction and
eliminating the lengthy time required to teach a new language
(Farid & McMahan, 2004; Wei, 2000).

Furthermore, during the military era the gap between
the rates of males and females attending schools remained
significant. General Barre challenged some cultural norms of
the Somalis. For the first time, the notion of keeping young
females at home and gender roles in general were challenged
(Abdikadir & Cassanelli, 2007; UNESCO, 1985). He
imported ideals of social justice from the Socialist System.
On the ground, however, materialization of these ideals
became remote due to community disapproval and lack of

27

"financial, educational, and human resources" (UNESCO, 1985).

As I mentioned earlier, the majority of Somalis are nomads, and the modern school systems were only available in the main cities. Thus many Somalis who grew up in the 1960s and early 1970s were not able to access education in Somalia. The alternative and often times the preferred schools, were Koranic schools. The number of religious-sponsored Koranic schools has remained higher than the number of government-sponsored primary schools throughout history. Although the Koranic schools were not compulsory, almost all children joined Koranic schools for rote instruction in Arabic before they attended primary education (UNESCO, 1985). Children learned to read Arabic only to memorize the Koran.

Excluding girls and women from educational circles and assigning them to an inferior social class is not inherently an Islamic tradition. In the Holy Koran, verse 124, chapter 4, the Almighty says "Whoever, be a male or female, does good deeds and he or she is a believer, then they will enter paradise." In Islam, men and women are dissimilar but equal. As a Somali who lived in Somalia during the 70s and 80s, I believe that patriarchal practices, lack of education, and men's desire to be dominant are what led to the unfortunate

28

situation of depriving women of education and a better future.

Purpose and Philosophy of Education in Somalia. Culturally, the purpose of schooling in both religious and government-sponsored schools has consistently been character formation alongside academic achievement. The emphasis on character, academics, and group identity were the products of an unprecedented marriage between Somali nomadic traditions, which emphasize group identity, and Islamic teachings, which emphasize the importance of knowledge and morality. The colonial structures of the Italian and British education systems, as well as Soviet communism, also influenced Somalia's education system. Character building, memorizing and reproducing information, as well as oral recitation, epitomized Somali education (Farid & McMahan, 2004).

Somalia's educational system philosophically emphasized the existence of a traditional canon of knowledge, which could be attained by only a few smart and hardworking people. This is similar to ancient Greek philosophy, and advocates the teaching of an essential body of knowledge that is deemed to be eternal and valid for all times and places, like the study of math, world languages, and Islamic studies. In Western terms, the study of Shakespeare and other classics are seen as important

29

knowledge. This is similar to the idealistic approach in which Plato contends that the learning focus will be subject matter (Johnson & Reed, 2008). Somali parents expect schools to teach their children world languages, math, science, reading, history, and current events.

In the Somali educational system, educators knew their subjects thoroughly, and the Socratic Method, which was not just a mere questioning but an interaction that exposes the gap in reasoning between the master or the teacher and the student through questions was the commonly accepted instructional method. Although this educational approach was accepted worldwide in past centuries, it defines teaching and learning narrowly and exclusively. In the U.S., similar traditional subject and teacher-centered approaches survived the pedagogical progressive movement of the early 20th century (Urban and Wagoner, 2009).

Educationists such as John Dewey and Paulo Freire, who believe that learners can produce knowledge with a reasonable amount of guidance, would starkly oppose the teacher-centered Somali education system. For Dewey, a teacher-centered classroom is a dry, lifeless, and counterproductive (Johnson and Reed, 2008). However, despite the global progressive student-centered movement, in Somalia, parents prefer the traditional teacher-centered

pedagogy that reflects the oral traditions of the Somali
culture.

Somali educators were hard workers with limited
resources. As a product of the Somali education system, I can
testify that Somali educators had passion for learning and
teaching. Their hard work and passion were not only natural,
but were also a professional requirement, as the field of
teaching and learning is dynamic in nature. Consequently,
Somali educators had to learn about their content area,
Eastern and Western teaching pedagogies, and strategies that
were continuously changing due to the country's status and to
the political orientations of the country. Exposure to different
political systems and pedagogies helped many Somalis to
become informed about the world, and prepared them to face
challenges abroad.

Admittedly, the ultimate goal for educating children
in Somalia was similar to the U.S.: to prepare children for
securing economic and social gains (Ogbu, 1978, p.19).
Somalis also value character, virtue, and morality. Training
students in rules of social conduct and nationalism were
important functions of schools. Somalis correlate the status of
the individual with his educational aptitude and attitude.
Historically, religious educators were most influential in
communities all over Somalia. They are called *Sheiks,*

Imams, Wadaad, and Fiqis. All titles indicate a level of respect. This approach is similar to the empiricists' philosophy of John Locke and Plato's ideal philosopher king. Somali educationists were not influenced directly by the philosophies of either Plato or Locke; yet, there are some similarities in their ideals that are worthy to be noticed.

Structure of the Somali Education System. Although Somali schools resembled Western organizations conceptually, Somali school infrastructure of early 1970s and 1980s was not like the sophisticated Western style. Desks, chairs, and blackboards were the only available resources. Unlike the U.S., Somali school governance was centralized and school management personnel, such as headmasters, reported to the Ministry of Education. Somali teachers and other school employees did not have unions. Under the Somali government of the 1970s and 1980s the collective power of workers was off-limits. The centralized Somali system did not allow flexibility and there was general fear that workers may take advantage of collective powers if they formed unions and the possibility that overall efficiency might be compromised. Similarly, in the West, today, some scholars contend that granting collective powers to employees would affect organizational efficiency negatively. "These collective strategies for noncooperation contribute to workers' willingness to display lack of motivation and perform at only minimal levels" (Lipsky, 1980, p. 17).

To put it bluntly, a hierarchal top-down management model characterized a typical Somali school system. Decisions and initiatives came from the top, the Ministry of Education to the school administration, and then down to teachers and other subordinates. This is an inherent structural characteristic of rational public administration theory (Weber, 1910). The Somali education system was characterized by hierarchy in which there is a supervision of lower offices by the higher ones. Hence, in Somali schools, teachers and other public employees were free as individuals, but as employees they had to follow directions, and implement policies initiated by their superiors. Unlike the American system, collective bargaining did not exist in Somalia during general Siyad's regime.

As far as teacher training was concerned, few teacher position candidates were selected on the basis of professional qualifications. Most teachers were poorly trained or not trained at all. Moreover, the Somali National University and other public colleges, which were part of the public institutions were looted and destroyed in the coups in 1991. However, a few for-profit universities and colleges were established in the late 1990s. In 2013, there are few trained teachers as the on-going war forced many former teachers to leave the country. Many Somali refugees who came to the U.S. previously lived in places where there were not functional education systems.

Classroom Setting/Dynamics. In the 1980s the city schools in Somalia had large classrooms with an average of more than 40 students in each classroom. In spite of the large number of children in one classroom with only one poorly trained teacher, behavioral issues never existed (UNESCO, 1985). According to Farid and McMahan (2004), given the high teacher-student-ratio, classroom management was the easiest part for teachers to deal with because students and parents perceived education as a privilege, and teachers and school administrators were able to expel or remove students from schools without due process.

In contrast, in U.S. schools, classroom management is a very important aspect of the teaching and learning process. In the U.S., most teacher preparation programs offer classroom management training and expect teacher interns to learn how to prevent and correct student misbehaviors. It is a subject for future studies to discuss whether the tranquility in the Somali classrooms was a superficial peace or students believed obedience was their moral obligation Physical punishment and suspensions from the school were acceptable preventive and corrective consequences for any infraction of the rules.

Role of Parents. Furthermore, parents' role in education was and continues to be limited to sending students to school. Parents expect educators to assume the role of preparing the children for a productive and rewarding adult life (Farid & McMahan, 2004). Teachers and other adults in the community were seen as shepherds or in western legalese "in loco parentis." Teachers advised, fed, and even disciplined children. Teachers are the most trusted members in Somali society, especially the ones who teach at the Koranic schools.

However, these unique educational and cultural characteristics did not prevent the Somali people from the bloody civil war in which hundreds of thousands lost their lives, millions were displaced internally, and millions more moved to all over the world as refugees. Many Somalis were resettled in major cities in the West including Toronto, London, Minneapolis, and Columbus. The cities of Portland and Lewiston, Maine also received a large number of Somali refugees.

Somalis in Diaspora. According to Somali community sources in the United States, there were more than 250,000 Somalis living in the U.S. in 2011. Some Somalis were resettled in Maine by government and non-profit agencies such as Catholic Charities of Maine, while others came to Maine as secondary immigrants after being settled in other states like Georgia. As a Somali refugee, I know that many Somalis who were seeking safe communities to raise their families moved from large cities, such as Atlanta and Chicago to Maine. Although there is no accurate count of the number of Somalis in Maine, community members estimate the number of Somalis in Greater Portland and Lewiston as close to 10,000.

Somali Community in Portland, Maine. Somali refugees admit that the scarcity of skilled and unskilled jobs in Maine was not enough to deter them from coming to Maine. The presence of good school and health care systems and the opportunity to raise children in low crime areas were sufficient reasons to move to Maine. The presence of their relatives, other ethnic Somali community members, and a "relatively generous public assistance" system were additional motives (Farid & McMahan, 2004; Ihotu, 2011). A recent study suggests that welfare is not the only reason why Somalis are coming to Maine (Hough, Heisman, Lanetheir, & Toner, 2011).

Arman and Kapeteijins (2004) highlighted that Somalis, who are culturally nomadic, like to travel and take on new challenges. They theorized that might be one of the

36

reasons that Somalis are moving from place to place. Traditionally, nomads continuously move their livestock to better grazing land. Somalis believe that moving from one place to another increases the chances of getting wealthy and gaining knowledge.

As a recent immigrant myself, I agree with Ihotu's speculation that the social and political attitudes of local communities attracted Somalis to come to and stay in Maine and similar states (Ihotu, 2011). In short, other than the unfamiliar temperate climate, for Somali refugees, Maine is considered a good place to be, and they view Mainers as tolerant and their political attitudes as progressive and pro-immigrant.

Challenges for Somalis in Maine. The influx of Somali refugees in Southern Maine has led to an influx of Somali students in schools. This contributes to financial and instructional challenges for the school systems, particularly in Portland and Lewiston. The integration of the students who are not familiar with the U.S. education system, and the incorporation of the needs of the students and their families into the traditional and rigid U.S. educational system are challenging for all. Preparing educators for teaching ELL students in sheltered or in mainstream classrooms is one of the immediate challenges. Other challenges include economic, political, and social.

Although we have various newspaper accounts and documentation on societal and governmental responses to the arrival of the newcomers, little is known or documented about how the local community has responded to the additional educational challenges presented by the new Mainers. However, studies conducted in the southern states show that immigrant, and language minority students are often unwelcome in their communities. Immigrant students and their families become unwanted and have been discriminated against because of their ethnicity and immigration status. In North Carolina, for example, Bacallao (2004) found that immigrant students faced "covert" and "overt" discrimination from their peers, and from school staff as well due to their perceived ethnic and immigration status (Bacallao, 2004; Machado-Cass, 2006).

As a Somali, I know firsthand that Somalis in Maine and elsewhere in the United States face many challenges. Learning a new language and culture, dealing with trauma, lacking education and job skills, and adjusting to the higher latitude climate are a few of the challenges Somali refugees are facing. However, raising children in the U.S. is most difficult aspect for Somali parents.

Ihotu (2011) argued that after 9/11 Muslim immigrants are in an unfortunate situation. "Socioeconomic and immigration status, race, and religious affiliation" could place Somalis in a position where their "integrity and intentions" are often questioned. For example, in 2002, the former Mayor of Lewiston, Maine, Larry Raymond declared publically, "The Somali community must exercise some discipline and reduce the stress on our limited finances ... Our city is maxed out financially, physically, and emotionally" (Maine Sunday Telegram, 2002). The current mayor of the same city, Bob MacDonald made a campaign promise in 2011 in which he stated that he will make the city "less attractive to layabouts and deadbeats many of whom do not speak English" (Bangor Daily News, 2011) Indeed, Somalis comprise the largest language minority group in Lewiston, and perceived that MacDonald's comments were directed at them. These are just local examples of how the integrity of Somali immigrants in the community is questioned (Ihotu, 2011).

In spite of the often negative feelings some citizens have about refugees and immigrants, local school systems recognize their obligation to provide an adequate education for all children who live within their limits. These obligations are defined in national policies and implemented in particular

39

programs. Individual states and localities have devised proactive policies to meet the learning needs of language minority students, and to create different teaching and learning models which are adopted in different municipalities and states (Garcia, 1994).

Schooling for English Language Learners

Policies and Legislation Related to ELL

In regard to ELL education, there are legal precedents that mandate the rights of ELL students to an education. Under the United Nations Convention of the Rights of the Child, every child is entitled to receive free education without discrimination "on account of race, color, sex, language, religion, political or other opinion, national or social origin, property, birth or other status, whether of himself or of his family" (United Nations , 1989). In the U. S., *Brown v. Board of Education of Topeka, Kansas Board of Education* (1954), the court ruled that segregation in public schools is a violation of the Fourteenth Amendment.

The 1973 case of *Lau v. Nichols* was another milestone ruling regarding ELL education. It is rooted in Title VI of the Civil Rights Act of 1964. In *Lau v. Nichols* all school-age children, regardless of their native language, were given the right to access theoretically sound education (Macswan & Rolstad, 2006). The law challenged the notion of treating ELL students like native speakers of English. According to the law "… there is no equality of treatment merely by providing [ELL] students with the same facilities, textbooks, teachers and curriculum" (U.S. Department of Education, 2013). According to Callahan & Dabach (2011), *Castaneda v. Pickard* (1981) augmented Lau. Under *Castaneda v. Pickard*, schools were mandated to place students appropriately and implement sound research based programs in all dimensions of the educative process including instruction and assessment. And in *Plyler v. Doe* (1982) the Supreme Court struck down a state statute denying funding for education to children who were illegal immigrants.

In *Dianna v. State Board of Education* (1970) the testing of ELL students in English and then placing them in special education settings was challenged. The court ruled that ELL students have the right to be tested in their native languages. Consequently, the Somali students in Portland, Maine have the right to an equitable education. However, Callahan & Dabach (2011) noted that there are gaps between the spirit of the laws regarding ELL education and their implementation and realization on the ground.

Implementation in Portland Public Schools

Somalis and other new immigrants are not aware of their rights, because they came from places where these rights did not exist. Also many of them have not been in the U.S. long enough to learn English which is essential for understanding and accessing educational opportunities for their children. In Portland, the Multilingual and Multicultural Office of Portland Schools is delegated to meet the demands of the newcomers and to implement the laws and regulations. The Multilingual handbook is comprehensive, and includes the district's Lau Plan. School personnel use the handbook as a guide. It informs staff about curricular, instructional, and other related services to ensure that all English Language Learners (ELLs) are getting quality education (Portland Public Schools, 2013).

To meet the needs of language minority students and families, Portland Public Schools established English as Second Language Programs as early as 1980. Portland Public Schools implements their version of a Lau Plan to meet the legal requirement and to serve students and their families, from school registration to monitoring students' academic achievement in mainstream classrooms. The Multilingual and Multicultural Center was established to oversee the implementation of these policies (Portland Public Schools, 2013). To be sure, it is not the intent of this study to evaluate Portland Schools, to evaluate whether there is a gap between practice and policies in the system. However, the system has a comprehensive Lau Plan in which policies, forms, accommodation, and assessment process can be found.

Experiences of Somali Students and Parents in Portland Public Schools

Little is known about the experiences and attitudes of Somali students in U.S. schools. However, my anecdotal observations as an educator in Portland schools, and a member of the Somali community in Portland, Maine, have given me an insider view of what Somali students are experiencing. In order to address the experiences and the attitudes of the youngsters and their parents, one should understand that not all Somali refugees living in the U.S. have similar backgrounds. For example, some children and parents experienced formal education before their arrival in the U.S., while many others had little to no schooling or even saw a school. Some were born to Somali parents in the U.S., others came to the country at younger ages and started elementary school in the U.S. Many others came as adolescents. In other words, drawing conclusions about the experiences of Somali students in Portland, Maine using Somali culture and language as conclusive predictors and measures of successes and failures without systematic study is very difficult, and may be inaccurate.

Traditionally, Somalis value education. Somali parents living in Portland want their children to excel in education. Children, especially adolescents, are expected to do well in school with little or no help from parents. At the age of fifteen, adolescents are considered adults in Islamic and Somali tradition. Parents feel they have discharged their responsibility if they enroll their kids in school and buy for them any school related materials they can afford. Beyond that, education and discipline belongs to the realm of the school. In short, some students' education suffers due to the conflicting parental and school expectations.

The relationships between Somali parents and their children are complicated and can range from disengaged to warm depending on acculturation and pre-settlement human capital. Some parents employ their cultural beliefs about child development, gender roles, and expectations. For example, in Islam, boys are considered to be men and girls as women at the age of fifteen. Some parents will consider their fifteen year old boys and girls as adults. However, I observed that some parents accept the Western concepts of child development, and treat their child accordingly. Many Somalis attend parent teacher conferences for their high school children. This practice was rare in Somalia. This is an indication that Somali parents are trying to learn about their new environment. Also, Somali children have figured out how to navigate the different and sometimes contradictory cultural and societal expectations and become bicultural, code switching as needed given the context (Cummins, 1996). They know how to conduct themselves when they are at home, and when they are with their peers and in the community. Recent arrivals continue to struggle with the transitions.

Along the same lines, Muslim children master how to conduct themselves in the Koranic schools. The Koranic classes are often held at the mosques. The teachers often receive monthly payments from parents. Almost all Somali children of ages five and older attend the Koranic schools for at least six hours on the weekends. Some parents send their children to the Koranic schools every day for at least two hours. In the following section, research findings on parental involvement and their effects on student achievement are presented.

Literature on Parental Involvement in Their Children's Education

Parental Involvement in General

Educators and institutions recognized that the one-dimensional teacher-centered approach was not in the best interest of the students (Epstein, 1996). After realizing that school and home cultures influence each other, creating mutual relationships between parents and schools and involving all families in the education of children of all ages has become the new best practice (Christensen & Sheridan, 2001; Crespo-Jimenez, 2010; Cutler, 2000).

The importance of parents' role in the education of children increased after Dr. Joyce Epstein proposed her theory of overlapping spheres of influence. She argues that schools must not only care about their students but they also need to extend similar care to the children's families. She suggests that educators view their students not only as students but also as children. (Epstein, 2001). She considers educators and parents as partners who share a single responsibility: educating the children. Epstein not only argues that there is a strong correlation between parent involvement and the development of students' aptitude and attitude but also suggested concrete ways schools can collaborate with parents regarding their children's education. According to Epstein, schools can help parents' understanding of child development, how to establish communication from and to schools, and how to help children with learning. Additionally, parents must be included in decision-making and governance processes (Epstein, 1996).

Some scholars took on the charge of defining the nature of the parents' role and the tasks parents need to perform in order to enhance their children's education. For instance, Senge, et al. (2001) correlated students' academic aptitude, confidence, and character to parents' involvement. According to Senge, parents must be involved in all aspects of schooling from teaching and helping with homework at home to volunteering and attending school events, to problem solving with the educators in order for students to gain the confidence they need to succeed.

Research shows that parent involvement is not only beneficial in student achievement, but also helps parents find joy in their children's performance, and educators and institutions become more efficient and effective (Christenson & Sheridan, 2001). However, how to involve all parents in the public education processes presents tremendous challenges, mainly due to the diversity in the population.

Contrary to the above mentioned theories and research findings which link student achievement to parents' involvement in school, Fan and Chen (2001) highlighted inconsistencies in how parental involvement is defined and measured. They questioned the definition of parental involvement and how parental involvement is measured.

Parental Involvement of Language Minority Parents

There is an overwhelming body of research suggesting positive correlation between parental involvement and students' academic achievement and their overall wellbeing (Crespo-Jimenez 2010), and there are factors, which influence parental involvement. Two main factors which influence parental involvement are socio-economic status and the educational attainment of the parents. Parents' level of education and schooling experiences influence their views on education and level of participation in their children's schooling. Many parents are not able to help their children with homework because they lack the required content knowledge (Floyd, 1998; Sosa, 1997). However, this is not unique to language minority populations. For example, parents who dropped out of school or never had formal education often cannot be involved in helping their children with their homework. Similarly, parents who are working long hours may not be able to attend school events. Culture and gender roles within different cultures are also considered as important factors. For example, in some societies women are not educated, and in turn, are not expected to help children with their school work when they had limited or no schooling themselves.

Culture and language also affect involvement of language minority parents in their children's schools (Arias & Morillo-Campbell, 2008). Research shows that some minority communities have their own definitions and perceptions of parental involvement. Latino parents, for example, define parental involvement as limited to helping children with their homework and nurturing them at home, while American educators define parental involvement as formal undertakings such as attending parent-teacher conferences and other school sponsored events (Crespo-Jimenez, 2010).

Other predictors of parental involvement include organizational culture and educators' attitudes and practices. These factors can influence parents' perceptions and predict their involvement (Epstein, 1993). Traditionally, parents tend to be involved when they believe there are roles which they can play. Critical theorists argue that school culture is socially constructed and mirrors the culture of the dominant groups. They argue that school culture is often exclusive, different from, and sometimes in conflict with the culture of the minorities and the poor and that can influence parents' perceptions and involvement (Crespo-Jimenez 2010).

Patterns of Latino Parental Involvement in Middle School: Case Studies of Mexican, Dominican, and Puerto Rican Families

In her doctoral dissertation, Mellie Crespo-Jimenez (2010) studied the patterns of Latino parental involvement in their children's school. The study focused on parents of middle school children. Her research involved three case studies which she combined into one study. She departed from the notion of treating all language minorities into one group. She investigated the patterns of Mexican, Dominican, and Puerto Rican parental involvement and the factors, which influence their involvement. She also compared and contrasted her findings with the current practice of treating all language minority students as one group. Crespo-Jimenez (2010) used the Theory of Planned Behavior to structure the study. The sample for her study consisted of nine parents: Three Mexican, three Dominican, and three Puerto Rican. Participants were selected on a voluntary basis. She used interviews in English and Spanish, observations, surveys, and studied the demographic and educational records of the families participating in the study. One of the important findings of this study was the misunderstanding between Latino parents and educators around the concept of parental roles and involvement. All participants expressed their willingness to improve their involvement even though they did not know how. However, they described the presence of some factors, which limited their involvement. They listed culture, language, parent's prior education, and organizational culture as some of the main limiting factors. The absence of communication between the schools and the parents is often a result of a language barrier which can lead to the perception in language minority communities that they are unwanted. Some of the participants in the study felt rejected and discriminated against because they could not find people who could communicate in their language. Some participants complained about their inability to help their children with the homework. As far as the culture is concerned, the participants of Crespo-Jimenez's study believed that they were involved in their children's education, which was evidenced by their willingness to participate when they were asked by the educators.

For my study, I adapted elements of the survey and the interview protocol of Crespo-Jimenez's study and applied them to a study of views on education and schooling, perceptions of involvement, and the factors which influence their involvement in schools of another language minority subgroup -- Somalis. Like Crespo-Jimenez's study, participants in my study are also parents of middle school children. The Theory of Planned Behavior (TPB) is used to situate and frame the design of this case study. Crespo-Jimenez (2010) used Ajzen's (1985) TPB to interpret parents' intentions and behavior to be (not to be) involved in their children's education. She suggests that past experiences of the parents and their perceptions of the views of those whom they value including community members can influence parents' decisions.

Conceptual Framework

The conceptual framework helped build the instruments and guide the analysis. It also provided a context in which to explain the data and interpret the findings of the study. This conceptual framework describes the major concepts in relationship to the three elements of the Theory of Planned Behavior: beliefs, normative behavior (subjective norms), and control beliefs (opportunities and barriers). Beliefs are often influenced by a person's life and educational experiences, while subjective norms are, often socially constructed. The central concept of the study is parental involvement of language minority parents in the public education system and the factors, which determine their involvement or lack of involvement. Components of the conceptual framework are established through a synthesis of prior research and literature in the area of parental

52

involvement in general, and parental involvement of language minorities in particular. The analysis of my findings directly addressed the research questions and the major components of the conceptual framework.

As I illustrated in the conceptual framework, the Theory of Planned Behavior explains how different aspects of a person's life can impact their behavior with regard to their child's schooling. Research shows that ability to understand English and prior education of the parent can influence his behavior. Similarly, availability of transportation, type of employment, community expectations, and the age of the child influence parents' intentions and behavior to take particular action or engage in a particular behavior (Crespo-Jimenez, 2010; Pena, 2000). Also, the influence of organizational culture of schools and educator's expectation, immigration status of the parent, culture, and parent's views on public education on language minority parents' behavior are part of the mix of elements that may affect parental involvement (Berry, Boski, & Kim, 1988; Epstein, 1996; Floyd, 1998; Garcia, 1994; Pedraza, Scribner & Young, 1999; Sosa, 1997).

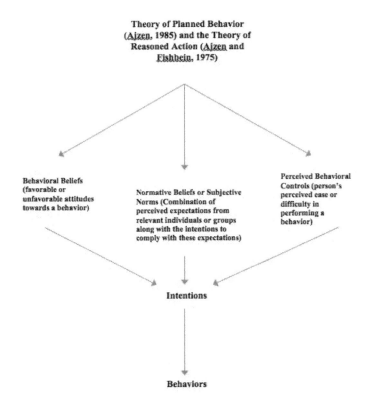

Figure 2.1. Conceptual Framework for Study, the Theory of Planned Behavior (Ajzen, 1985).

The Theory of Reasoned Action (TRA) was proposed by Martin Fishbein and Icak Ajzen in 1975 (Fishbein, Triandis, Kanfer, Becker, Middlestadt & Eichler, 2001). The theory links behavioral beliefs, and normative beliefs (subjective norms) to intentions and behavior. The theory is derived from the social psychology field. The components of TRA are three general constructs: behavioral intention (*BI*), attitude (*A*), and subjective norm (*SN*). According to TRA, an individual's behavior is a function of his perceptions about the behavior and subjective norms.

Theory of Planned Behavior (TPB) not only considers behavioral beliefs and normative beliefs, but also perceived control beliefs. Behavioral beliefs measure a person's relative (favorable or unfavorable) attitude to perform a behavior. For this research, "behavioral beliefs" is an indication of parents' readiness to be involved in their children's education and schooling. Attitude (favorable and unfavorable) consists of perceptions and beliefs about the consequences of performing the behavior influenced by parent's evaluation of these consequences. (Fishbein & Ajzen, 1975). The framework demonstrates that parents' decision to become involved (or not) in the education and the schools of their middle school age children can be influenced by a number of factors including parents' perceptions about parenting, teaching and teachers, and child development.

A subjective norm is seen as a combination of perceived expectations from relevant individuals or groups along with the intentions to comply with these expectations. In other words, parents' perceptions of and beliefs about the people who are important to them and what behaviors are socially accepted by those important or significant people influence their behaviors (Fishbein & Ajzen, 1975).

Parents' perceived ease or difficulty of demonstrating a specific behavior is also an important construct of this theory. To put the definition into simple terms: A person's voluntary behavior is predicted by her beliefs about that behavior, how she thinks other people would view her if she performed the behavior, and her perception about existing barriers and available opportunities for performing the behavior. A person's attitude, combined with subjective norms and perceived control of the person form his behavioral intention. For example, parents may believe that school is important for their children, but are not sure how the educators will react if they get involved, especially if culturally, the role of parents is to wait for the school to ask for input or request a specific action. Such parents expect schools to ask them to be involved in specific ways. Crespo-Jimenez's study (2010) has shown that intention does not always lead to actual behavior. Regardless of a person's intentions, other factors including time and ability to take action might influence a person's behavior.

The significance of using TPB for the framing of this study is its relation to an individual's intention to perform a behavior not only to her perceptions and subjective norms, but also to the amount of control the individual possesses of all factors affecting the actual performance of the behavior. In other words, both perceived behavior and environmental factors are used to predict behavior. For example, if a parent wants to be involved in her child's school and believes it to be important, but there are some barriers which do not allow her to be involved. Time, prior education, ability to speak English, and lack of transportation are some potential barriers.

Now that I have explained the organization of my conceptual framework, the following chapter will present an overview of the method and describe how a case study approach is the most appropriate method to address my research questions, create the sample of participants, and collect, manage and analyze data. It also explains my role as the researcher.

CHAPTER THREE
METHODOLOGY

The purpose of the proposed case study is to explore perceptions of the parents of Somali children who are in Portland Public Schools regarding education and schooling of their children and the perceptions and attitudes of these parents regarding their involvement in their children's education and schooling. This chapter provides the research questions, definitions of the key terms, a rationale for the design, the criteria for selecting participants, data collection and analysis procedures, and issues of validity and trustworthiness.

Research Questions

RQ 1. How do first generation Somali parents of middle school students who are part of a refugee population settled in Portland, Maine view education and schooling?

RQ 2. How are first generation Somali parents who are part of a refugee population settled in Portland, Maine involved in their middle school children's education in general and schooling in particular and what factors influence their involvement?

RQ 3. What are the perceptions of Somali parents of middle school students who are part of a refugee population settled in Portland, Maine whose children are or have been part of English Language Learners (ELL) programs with regard to the expectations of their children and the responsibilities of parents in the school?

Operational Definitions of Key Terms in the Research Questions

For the purpose of this study, the following operational definitions apply:

First generation: being the first generation of a family to reside in a particular country.

Somali parents: adults who live in Portland, Maine and have students in Portland Public Schools and are from Somalia, a country located in the Horn of Africa. It is the site of civil wars since 1988.

English language Learners: English Language Learners (ELL) are school-age children whose first language is not English and who are in the process of learning English. Students with this designation and their families receive some services including language services.

Education: the act of preparing children intellectually for a productive life. It encompasses many aspects of the educative process of children including public and religious schooling.

Schooling: institutionalization of education in grades and with a set of curriculum

Refugees: an individual "owing to a well-founded fear of being persecuted for reasons of race, religion, nationality, membership of a particular social group or political opinion, and living outside the country of his nationality, and unable to, or owing to such fear, is willing to avail himself of the protection of that country" (UNHCR, 2014). Somalia has been the site of civil wars since 1988.

Parental Involvement: parental work with children in education, and in schools and with educators to make sure their children succeed.

Middle School Students: students in grades six to eight.

The first research question was designed to explore Somali parents' views about schooling, and their experiences with schools. This allowed me to identify the parents' beliefs about education and schooling and subjective norms about schooling as related to their behavioral intentions (Ajzen, 1975).

The second question addressed the extent to which Somali parents are involved in the education and schooling of their children. In other words, the aim of the first and second research questions was crafted to gain knowledge about the participants and their views about parental involvement in education and schooling, and what factors influenced Somali parents' decisions to be involved in their children's education and schooling. This question illuminated the subjective norms, and the opportunities and barriers that are considered in the TPB as they influence the ability of parents to follow through on their behavioral intentions (Ajzen, 1985).

The third question addressed the expectation of Somali parents for their children and from the schools and their perceived responsibilities as parents. This question was focused on participants' expectations from relevant individuals or groups such as community members and educators of their children, and their intentions to comply with these expectations. This question addressed the subjective norm as it influences the intentions and the behavior of parents from a cross-cultural perspective. However, I realized during the second phase of the study that none of the interviewees had children in English Language Learners (ELL) programs. All five participants reported that their children were born in the U.S. and had never been enrolled in the ELL programs of Portland Public School. So, I have to admit that the process and the collected data do not address elements of the third research question. Nevertheless, I collected some data relevant to this population's perceptions with regard to the expectations of their children and the responsibilities of parents in the school, which I share in the following chapters.

Design

This research followed a case study design. The method of case study research remains essential in many fields of social science inquiry, and is used to understand the experiences of individuals and communities (Yin, 2003). Methodological literature addresses case study research less than other qualitative research methods. However, in education and in similar social service fields, people and programs are optimally studied as cases in order to draw similarities to other persons and programs or highlight their uniqueness (Stake, 1995). Case study research design is used to define broad topics, to contextualize complex conditions, and to triangulate field evidence (Yin, 2003). The current research questions required general understanding. This general understanding was achieved by studying individual cases and interpreting experiences from the participants' expressed perceptions (Stake, 1995).

The data for the case study came from surveys and interviews. Both instruments were designed to identify the perceptions of first generation Somali parents about U.S. education and schooling and how these perceptions influence parents' involvement in their children's education. Phase 1 of the study consisted of a survey of 20 parents. The second phase was a series of three interviews of each of five parents. The five participants were randomly selected from the 20 participants from the first phase.

Table 3.1. Theory of Planned Behavior Alignment with
Research Questions

Theory of Planned Behavior Components	Research Question 1	Research Question 2	Research Question 3
Beliefs	X	•	•
Subjective Norms	•	X	•
Behavioral Control	•	X	•
Intention and Behavior	X	X	•

Note. Table 3.1 is a representation of how Theory of Planned
Behavior (TPB) is related to the research questions. An X

indicates the research question addresses the component of TPB directly, whereas, a dot shows the research question addresses the component of TPB indirectly (inferred).

Sample

The participants in this study were Somali parents who have middle school children in public schools in Portland, Maine. It is important to note that this study was focused on a relatively small number of Somali refugee or former refugee parents. I acknowledge the possibility of variation within the Somali group as individuals have different experiences.

Many factors were considered when determining the number of participants for this dissertation study in order to increase the validity of the subsequent findings. The sampling technique was purposeful. I approached potential participants at mosques and at their homes. The population of this study was limited to parents of middle school children in Portland schools. Twenty parents (13 women and 7 men) who have children in one of the three middle schools in Portland were given a survey. Only five participants (two men and three women) of the original twenty were interviewed.

The number of female participants in the study was more than the number of males because most of Somali

66

parents are single women. Many Somali men lost their lives in the civil war or stayed back to care for their other relatives, while women and children were resettled by aid agencies in other countries. However, children of the participants who volunteered to be interviewed were born in the United States.

Recruitment

Before the study took place, the study and its goals, the consent forms, the interview protocol, and the survey were reviewed with community members who are able to read and write in Somali and in English (Appendix E). The goal of using community reviewers was to produce tools and documents that are culturally and linguistically appropriate.

To conduct a purposive sample that was representative of the population, I, in community centers and in their residences personally approached 50 participants, and a detailed description of the study and its goals were shared with them (Appendix A). The first 20 volunteers were given the survey. Somali parents with middle school students who attend one of the three middle schools in Portland, Maine fit the criteria. Participants who volunteered for the study completed a written consent form (Appendix B) and then responded to the survey. From this group of respondents, I recruited participants for the interview phase of the study. The goal was to have 20 participants in the first phase of the study, and five participants (of the 20) in the second phase of the study.

In order to accurately represent the perceptions and experiences of Somali parents of middle school children, diversity within the sample was considered. In addition to gender, prior education, ability to understand and speak English, and type of employment were considered for the survey to enhance diversity of the sample. However, it is important to keep in mind that there are no data to support that the sample selection criteria are representative other than my rough estimations. For example, no data are available about the number of Somali parents who understand and speak English or the percentage of Somalis parents who have any level of formal education.

Generally, recruiting Somali parents was not an easy task because of the nature of their jobs. Many Somali men drive taxis or work long hours and have limited time for other engagements. Somali women in Maine are mostly single mothers who work and care for their children, and sparing time to be part of a study was hard for them. To show respect and interest to the participants, I spent a fair amount of time with the participants before each interview because, by custom, I have to have tea and talk about different things before I get down to the purpose of the visit. Additionally,

Somali mothers hesitated to be part of any study because of the fear that their identities could be disclosed. To protect the identities of the participants, pseudonyms were used as identifiers, and lists and date were placed in a secure place. No financial remuneration was provided out of respect, as that would violate a cultural norm.

Instruments

Survey. In this study, the survey was the first phase. I wanted to gather detailed data on Somali parents' views of education and schooling to provide context for the interviews. The purpose was not to generalize to a large population of Somalis in the United States, but to capture the views and perceptions of the participants in this case study in Portland, Maine. The twenty participants were given a survey to address research question number two: How are first generation Somali parents who are part of a refugee population settled in Portland, Maine involved in their middle school children's education in general and schooling in particular and what factors influence their involvement? (Appendix D). The survey was designed to address the three elements of the Theory of Planned Behavior (Ajzen & Fishbein, 1980) with questions that address behavior, intention, and context. The survey was available for the participants in Somali and English languages. A Likert scale

69

was used for measurement. The instrument had questions related to the influence of identity and culture on parental involvement. It also revealed what other factors (outside of participants' control) influence his or her decision to become involved (or not) in schooling. The survey elicited responses from a sample size of 20 for good representation of various perspectives. Interviews were conducted for greater depth of understanding from a smaller sample size.

Interviews. In the second phase of the study, the perceptions and experiences of five Somali parents in Portland, Maine whose children are in Portland public middle schools were captured. One-to-one interviews of the five participants were conducted to address all research questions. However, research questions one and two, and parts of research question three were directly addressed in the interview phase. All interviews took place in the homes of the participants.

The open-ended interview questions were the best tools to explore the perspectives of participants. Every participant was interviewed using an interview protocol (Appendix E) for at least one hour for the first interview. I conducted three interview phases as Seidman (2006) suggests. In the first interview, I asked participants about their lives and context in the light of education and schooling. In the second interview, participants were asked about their

70

present experiences in their children's education and schooling. In the third interview, participants were asked about the meaning of their experiences. In other words, the interview questions were designed to highlight the participants' contexts and their experiences and to solicit from participant's reflections on their perceptions, expectations, and experiences (Seidman, 2006). One of the advantages of semi-structured interviews was that I had the opportunity to interpret and ask participants clarifying questions in their own language, Somali. Also, participants could ask clarifying questions.

The open-ended interview style was the most appropriate approach. It allowed me as the researcher to listen to the views and the experiences of the participants (Creswell, 2006). The interview protocol was available in English and Somali depending on participants' choice. Periods between the semi-structured interviews allowed me to construct specific probing questions, which were grounded in the theoretical framework of the study, and were derived from what participants responded previously. These probing questions were recorded in the final transcripts of the study. All interviews were audio recorded and field notes were taken for later analysis.

The first interview was designed to explore the context of the lives of the participants as it relates to their own education and schooling experiences and their perceptions and expectations about parental involvement in children's education and schooling. Interview questions were also designed to elicit their experiences as parents of middle school children in Portland, Maine. The data collected in this stage addressed most directly behavioral beliefs about schooling and education as they relate to intentions and behavior as defined as constructs within the Theory of Planned Behavior.

The second interview involved asking participants a set of questions about their current behaviors and actions as parents in schools. Participants were asked to describe their expectations of schooling and their experiences while dealing with U.S. public education. Then they were asked to compare and contrast their experiences as students and their expectations of schools to the experiences of their children's schooling, Participants were asked directly and indirectly whether they perceive they have control over participating in their children's education. Asking participants about their perceptions and the contextual issues which influence their involvement in their children's education addressed social norms, perceived controls, and environmental factors that

72

Ajzen addressed when he modified the TPB from the original TRA (Ajzen, 1985).

The one-hour follow-up interviews were conducted to ensure that all research and interview questions were answered, to ask for clarification of any answers, and to conduct a member check on the researcher's interpretation of the meaning of responses. Also, I encouraged the participants to reflect on what they had said and offer further explanation or elaboration after having gone through the process of articulating their understanding. The member check of interpretations of earlier interviews helped to increase validity of the research data.

The following table represents the alignment of the research instruments with the research questions. The survey was completed by twenty participants, and the series of three interviews were completed by five participants.

Table 3.2. Alignment of the Survey and the Interview

Protocols with the Research Questions

	RQ1	RQ2	RQ3

Survey	•	•	X
First Interview	•	•	X
Second Interview	X	•	X
Third Interview	X	X	X

Note. Table 3.2 is a representation of how the survey and the interview protocol were related to the research questions. A dot indicates that the question was directly addressed in the instrument. X Indicates the question was inferred from answers to the instrument.

Table 3.3. Alignment of Research Questions with Theory and
Instrumentation

Theory of Planned Behavior Components	Survey	Interview Protocol
		Biographical info and description of education
Beliefs Q1 and Q2	What is the purpose of education? Educational experience and experiences related to helping child with school, involvement in school.	Experiences related to helping child with school, involvement in school
Intention and Behavior Q1 and Q2	What are intentions regarding involvement in schooling? What are barriers?	What does parental involvement mean to you?
Subjective Norms Q1, Q2, and Q3	Attitudes of others including educators and children regarding parental involvement in education and schools.	Participant's childhood and parental involvement, community norms and willing to comply with these norms, child attitude regarding parental involvement, organizational culture, and desire to participate in spite of barriers.

Data Management

Confidentiality is very critical in the field of research. As the researcher, I took purposeful steps to keep participants' identities and responses confidential. I explained my proposal and plan to project participants. All participants signed written informed consent and were assured that their identities and their children's identities would not be disclosed. I substituted names with codes for identification, and I placed codes and all data in a secure location. The data was translated, transcribed, and analyzed within five days after collection. Accuracy and the reliability increase when data are transcribed into written form immediately (Seidman, 2006). I did not use a professional transcriber to help transcribe. The data were secured in password-protected files on my computer while I was still collecting data. In the final report, pseudonyms were assigned to participants and to their children's schools. Additionally, all collected information and data were destroyed five months after the study was completed.

The data obtained from the surveys informed and created context for the interviews. I followed quantitative traditional methods to interpret the survey data. I presented the survey results in table and graphs, and in descriptive form. All interviews were audio-recorded and the initial reactions to the interview were documented within 48 hours. Transcripts of each interview were quickly translated from Somali to English, transcribed, and analyzed to answer the research questions and to explore further questions and themes for the next interview. Interviews were spaced to allow time for the previous data to be translated, transcribed, and analyzed in preparation for the next phase.

Data Analysis

Initially, the data analysis process was dynamic and inductive and started during field work. The goal was to capture participants' stories and to identify themes within their narratives. Transcripts and field notes were analyzed for patterns that led to themes (McMillan & Schumacher, 2010). The process of coding for themes highlighted the relationship between participants' stories and Somali parents' views on parental involvement in the education and schools of their children.

After the inductive analysis, data were analyzed deductively. I used my research questions and the framework of TPB: beliefs, subjective norms, and perceived behavioral controls to analyze data deductively. During this phase of data analysis, I developed codes and placed them in a matrix with components of the conceptual framework. Direct quotes (key words or phrases) from the transcripts were placed in the matrix as well. Also, the data was inductively coded based on what had arisen that was outside the theories and conceptual framework. For example, interviewees brought issues related to safety and school transportation.

I attempted to understand interviewees' perspectives and categorized their responses using constructs of TPB. Even though my interview protocol and survey questions were designed to address beliefs, subjective norms, and perceived behavioral controls and how they shape intentions and behaviors of the research participants, it was not an easy task to conclude that intentions and behavior/lack of behavior of the five interviewees were direct results of one construct. For example, Rahma and Dowlo expressed their beliefs and experiences regarding parental involvement in schools, yet their behaviors are opposite to their beliefs. While other all interviewees reported that their community members expect them to be involved in their children's education, for most of them that was not translated into behaviors. Therefore, the theory did not provide a complete picture because the descriptions provided by the participants were not linear: The three factors did not necessarily combine to lead to intentions and behaviors. There were other factors that surfaced that also influenced the intentions and behaviors, namely emotions.

In summary, the data analysis stemmed from information provided by the participants in responding to questions in the survey and during semi-structured interviews. The data obtained from the survey were analyzed using traditional survey analysis processes while referencing the research questions and conceptual framework and interpreting the results. The data obtained from the interviews were presented first in a narrative format. A thematic analysis of the narrative section provided details and insights about the perceptions these participants have about their schooling, their involvement in their children's schools, and their own experiences. The thematic analysis was useful in connecting the individual narrative to the collective story of the participants through the research questions and conceptual framework of the study (Stake, 1995).

Trustworthiness

I have certain advantages as a Somali teacher in the Portland Public Schools because I understand both cultures. Usually, I am not surprised nor challenged by the degree of misunderstanding, cultural differences, and conflict that takes place between Somali parents and educators. I work closely with other educators in order to promote culturally sensitive practices and minimize the effects of negative perceptions that could lead to the educational practices that reinforce the

79

assumptions about language minority students and their parents. In many cases my designated role as a teacher changes to a role of cultural broker. I find myself bridging different and sometimes contradictory cultural norms and practices in many aspects of schooling processes. Even though this research was situated in a particular place it has value as a case study that can inform other educators of Somali students and also shows what U.S. educators need to consider when working with ELL students.

Interviewing as a method of research has its advantages and disadvantages. Allowing subjects to reconstruct their experiences and express their views can be achieved by interviews. (Seidman, 2006). Yet, I recognize my potential bias in all stages of the research, including the fieldwork stage. Although extra care was required at the analysis and interpretation stage, I examined my role as researcher throughout the entire process by allowing the data to emerge from the participants, worked intentionally to limit my familiarity with the circumstances, and my inner latent feelings as a native of Somalia and as a teacher in the Portland Public Schools not to personally influence the research process.

Additionally, I like to think I have a certain advantage as I identify myself as a former refugee, a Somali, a Muslim, a member of the target population, and above all one who maintains a strong connection with the community. My identity and connection allowed me to understand and capture language nuances and feelings. These advantages added values and efficiency to the research method. However, I was aware how my identity and status could present both benefits and challenges to the process. Potentially, my identity could limit my objectivity and become a potential source of bias. Moreover, my position in the community as a teacher and a leader could be another limitation as some participants may have said things to please me given the context. Many Somalis in Portland, Maine ask me for ideas about education and in other domains as I am - so far- the only certified Somali teacher in the state of Maine, and a relatively highly educated individual. It is certain that participants sought my input during the interview process. That increased the potential risk of bias. However, I was able to strike a balance between being a community member and advocate, and a researcher. Therefore I had to ensure that my personal experiences and attitudes were not influencing the research processes. I bracketed my feelings and biases by recording what I was hearing and finding in a journal during the entire process. I also consulted and shared situations with my advisor. In addition to above-mentioned measures, I followed Institutional Review Board (IRB) guidelines.

In the next three chapters I present the results of the data analysis and prepare a narrative to present the findings. In the report, the emerging themes related to the existing literature were compared and contrasted. I also articulated recommendations and limitations in the final chapter. However, caution should be taken not to ascribe the findings from the study to a larger immigrant population as the study took place in one selected site with a small number of participants.

CHAPTER FOUR

PRESENTATION OF THE DATA

The purpose of this research was to explore perceptions of the parents of Somali children who are in Portland Public Schools regarding education and schooling of their children and the perceptions and attitudes of these parents regarding their involvement in their children's education and schooling. While Chapters 1 and 2 provided an introduction and review of the literature, Chapter 3 focused on the methodologies employed and the research design. This chapter focuses on presentation of the data collected during the study. The chapter begins with a brief introduction followed by presentations of the quantitative and the qualitative data: surveys and semi-structured interviews respectively. The mixed method approach has merit over other single method studies because together qualitative and quantitative data because it captures different data sets. (Creswell, 2007)

In the quantitative section, I rely on the theoretical framework of the Theory of Planned Behavior (TPB) to organize the data. According to the Theory of Planned Behavior, any intention or/and behavior (or lack of intention and/or behavior) is the result of the combination of a person's beliefs about the behavior, social pressure, and perceived control, which refers to the perceived ease or difficulty in performing the behavior. These data are presented in three sections which are: a) the beliefs of survey respondents towards education and schooling; b) the beliefs of survey respondents about the norms and the expectations of others and how these normative beliefs influence their intentions and behaviors regarding their parental involvement and; c) the survey respondents' perceived ease or difficulties of being involved in their children's schools.

To report the qualitative interview data, I introduce the interviewees. Long statements and quotes from the interviews are used to present the background information of participants, their educational history, their involvement in their children's education, and their views on and involvement in their children's education and schooling.

Survey Results

A 20 question multiple choice and open-ended survey (Appendix D) was administered to 20 Somali parents (13 women and 7 men) who have middle school children in Portland Public Schools. The subjects were selected on a voluntary basis. I went to the mosques in Portland, Maine to meet individually with 50 Somali parents who have middle school children in the public schools and described my research to them. Later, thirty-four written invitations with descriptions of the process in both English and Somali were sent to the participants who showed interest in participating. The first 20 participants were given the surveys in paper form in person. The results of the surveys are presented in the following sections.

Parents' Perception About Education and Schooling

Somali parents of middle school children who took the survey believe parent participation in education and in public and religious schools is very important. Figure 4.1 shows parents' beliefs about the importance of parent participation in education and public and religious schooling. As you will see later in the qualitative data, Somali parents indicate they view public education as a means of ensuring better financial gain, while they view religious education as a moral obligation.

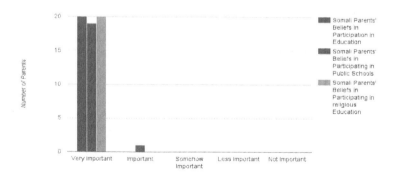

Figure 4.1. Beliefs of Somali Parents about the Importance of Parental Involvement in Education and Schooling

Normative Beliefs of Somali Parents

Normative beliefs are the second component of TPB. According to TPB, normative or subjective norms influence an individual's intention and subsequent behavior. In the survey, parents were asked about external factors which they think influence their intentions and beliefs. The three specific things they were asked were: a) their perceptions about whether the public and the religious teachers of their children expect them to be involved in their children's school; b) their perception about the expectations of Somali community members in Portland, Maine regarding their parental involvement and; c) their perceptions of how their own middle school children view their involvement in their schools.

Figure 4.2 indicates that only 50% of the 20 parents strongly agree that the teachers of their children in the public schools want them to participate in the schools, while 95% of the same parents strongly agree that the religious schoolteachers want them to participate in their children's religious school. As far as the community influence is concerned, 70% of the survey respondents strongly agree that their community members expect them to be involved in their children's education and schooling.

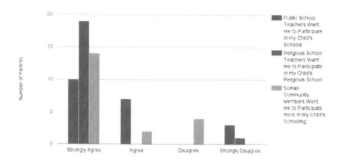

Figure 4.2. Somali Parents' Perceptions of Behavioral Expectations from Relevant Groups

A child's attitude toward his or her parent's involvement is an important factor in parental involvement. In the survey, parents were also asked about their children's attitudes towards their participation. Figure 4.3 shows that only 20% of the parents strongly agree that their children do not want them to be involved in their religious education, while the percentage of parents who strongly agree that their children do not want them to be involved in their public schools is 50%, and 40% of the same parents strongly agree that their middle school children do not want them to be involved in their education at all.

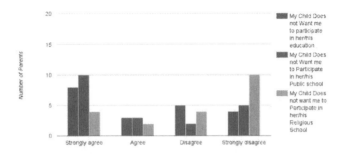

Figure 4.3. Somali Parents' Perceptions about their
Children's Attitudes Regarding their Parental Involvement.

Perceived Controls

According to the TPB, perceived ease or difficulty of performing a specific action is an important factor in influencing one's intention or behavior. As figure 4.4 indicates, almost 60% of the parents who responded to the survey reported the existence of opportunities (very often, often, or sometime) for their participation in their children's public schools. However, 70% of the same parents reported the existence of barriers (very often, often, or sometimes) to their parental involvement in the public schools of their children. In the qualitative section of the study, participants who were interviewed talked about these perceived controls.

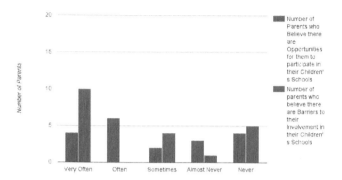

Figure 4.4. Opportunities for and Barriers to Parental
Involvement of Somali Parents

Somali Parents' Intentions Regarding Parental Involvement

Figure 4.5 shows that Somali parents who took the survey not only believe that participation in education and schools of their children is very important, but they also desire to become more involved. In other words, their beliefs about the importance of education, the subjective norms, and behavioral controls are translated into intentions. The survey results show that all 20 parents who took the survey reported that they hope to participate and increase their current level of participation in the schools of their children. However, it is

another thing whether these intentions are translated into
behavior.

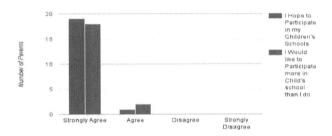

Figure 4.5. Intentions of Somali Parents Regarding
Involvement in Schools

Somali Parents' Behaviors Regarding Parental
Involvement

According to TPB, parents' perceptions of
participation in education and schools, subjective norms, and
perceived controls regarding parental involvement influence
their involvement or lack of involvement. Figure 4.6 shows
almost 60% of the Somali parents who took the survey said
that they very often or often visit the public schools of their
children regularly, while 25% sometimes visit the schools.
However, 100% of the same parents reported that they visit
(very often or often) their children's religious schools. There
are many potential reasons for the variation between parents'
visitation to public and religious schools. However, parents'

perceptions about teachers' attitude is one of the reasons. As
you see in figure 4.4, 90% of the parents strongly agree that
religious schoolteachers want them to be involved in the
school, while only 50% of the same parents strongly agree
the same about the public school teachers.

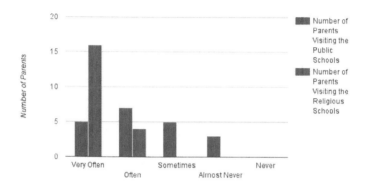

Figure 4.6. Somali Parents' Involvement in their Children's
Schools

Figure 4.7 shows the type of activities related to
children's education in which Somali parents of middle
school children indicate they participate. Almost 100% of
Somali parents of middle school children who took the
survey report they attend parent-teacher conferences at the
children's religious and public schools and talk to their
children about education. Eighty percent of the same parents

helped their children with Koranic homework from the religious schools. Also 60% of the parents reported that they help their children with their public school homework, secure academic assistance for their children, and transport them to athletics, playgrounds, and libraries. Very few say they attend school field trips and events or volunteered in the classrooms of their children.

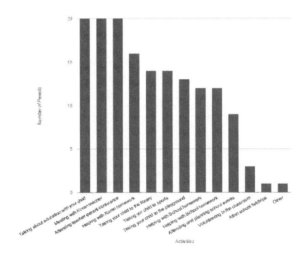

Figure 4.7. How Somali Parents Participate in their Children's Education

When the parents were asked to rank certain activities according to their importance, the majority of the Somali parents who took the survey ranked as their top priorities talking to their children about education in general and about religious education specifically, helping their children with their homework, and attending parent-teacher conferences. Getting academic assistance for their children and taking them to the libraries and sports were ranked second. Very few ranked "attending school events and field trips" as their priorities. However, after discussing with my advisor, I decided not to present the data as ranked, because many of the parents selected the same rank for multiple activities. For example, many parents put "talking to the children about education"; "helping their children with their homework"; and "attending parent-teacher conferences" as their first priority so I represented the data with a frequency count instead.

Summary of the Survey Data

The survey data were categorized according to the TPB framework. The survey data show how this sample of Somali parents of middle school students view education and schooling; how social pressure can influence Somali parents' intentions and behavior; and how perceived control influence their participation in their children's education and schooling. Also, the data show how Somali parents of middle school children report on their involvement in their children's education in terms of the activities.

Beliefs

According to the survey data, Somali parents who responded to the survey regard participation in their children's education as very important. Similarly, they viewed schooling (public and religious) as very important.

Subjective Norms

The parents who took the survey reported the presence of social pressure both supporting and discouraging participation of parents in their children's education and schooling. The data show that Somali parents believe that religious schoolteachers and their community members want them to be involved in their children's schooling. When it comes to the expectation of the public school teachers, only half of Somali parents strongly agree that public school teachers want them to participate in their children's schools. Also, the parents generally believe that their middle school aged children do not want them to participate in their public education.

Perceived Behavioral Control

The parents who responded to the survey reported the existence of some barriers and opportunities to their participation in their children's schools. I was able to ask the participants in the qualitative phase of the study about these perceived controls and how they influenced their parental involvement.

Intentions

The above mentioned beliefs, subjective norms, and perceived controls shape Somali parents' intentions regarding their participation in their children's schools. According to TPB, parents' views about education, social pressure, and the perceived behavioral controls shape their intentions. All survey respondents indicated that they hope to and would like to participate in their children's schools more than they do now.

Behavior

Despite obstacles, Somali parents indicate they participate in their children's education and schools in both academic and non-academic activities. The majority of those surveyed help their children with their homework, find academic assistance for their children, take the children to libraries, and attend parent-teacher conferences. They also talk to their children about the importance of education and take them to playgrounds and sports events. Additionally, the data show that all Somali parents who took the survey go to the religious school of their children more than they go to the public schools of their children. However, a majority of the Somali parents of middle school age students feel that their children do not want their parents to be involved in their schools. Few Somali parents surveyed participate in organizing and attending school events and fieldtrips.

Interviews of Somali Parents of Middle School Children

In the second phase of the study, five Somali parents were recruited from the original 20 to be interviewed. They were the first five who accepted the invitation to participate in this phase of the study. Table 4.1 presents demographic data of the participants who were interviewed. All participants were Somali parents of middle school children. Two of the female participants graduated from secondary schools (one in Somalia and the other outside of Somalia). The other one attended middle school in Somalia. Two participants are single parents. The two male participants graduated from universities prior their resettlement in the United States. One of the participants took language classes in an adult education program in the U.S. All participants live in housing projects in different neighborhoods in Portland. All participants are naturalized American citizens. The children attend the three different middle schools in the city indicated by letters A, B, or C.

Table 4.1. Participants' Demographic Information

Participant	Gender	Marital Status	Educational Attainment	Gender of student	School	Birth-place of Student
Dowlo	Female	Married	Attended middle school in Somalia	Male	C	USA
Rahma	Female	Single	High school diploma from Somalia	Male	A	USA
Idil	Female	Single	High school diploma from Pakistan	Female	A	USA
Jama	Male	Married	University degree from Egypt	Male	C	USA
Farah	Male	Married	University degree from Somalia	Male	B	USA

Every participant was interviewed three times following Seidman's (2006) interview model. The interview protocol was developed beforehand but was semi-structured. (Appendix E). The presentation of the data from the interviews is structured by presenting participants' background information, their perceptions about education and schooling, and their involvement in their children's education and schooling. The information included in the participants' information is important because it contextualizes participants' intentions and behaviors. Long statements and quotes from the interviews are included in this section. Fictitious names were given to participants to protect their identity.

In deciding how to order the presentation of the profiles, I used a continuum of satisfaction of parents with their children's public schools. I present the data starting with the person who voiced the most dissatisfaction, Dowlo, to the person who voiced the least dissatisfaction, Farah. I interviewed all participants in the Somali language and translated the transcripts to English.

Dowlo

Dowlo was born in Somalia where she completed middle school. She came to the United States as a refugee in 1996. She lives with her husband and three children. All of her children were born in the U.S. Like all the other interview participants, Dowlo lives in a public housing project. At the start of our interview, she told her children to respect the guest and lower their voices. She also silenced her mobile telephone.

Dowlo was orphaned by age 13. Her father left her mother when she was very young, and her mother passed away by the time she completed the middle school. Even though she did not go to school in the U.S., after she immigrated to the United States, she was able to learn English from coworkers and the community. At parent-teacher conferences, she did not ask for interpreters. "I speak English. It is my second language. I understand most of the time. I learned it in here. From the people." "I use my English. I never asked for interpreter. The schools offer me the option when they call me. Other times they do not ask me. When I go they do not."

Dowlo's mother was involved in her education.

> My mother was part of my education. My parents were not together. I was with my mother my entire life. Mother died before when I finished my intermediate school. My mother used to buy me all my needs for the school. She bought me uniforms and books.

She helped me with everything. She was involved and wanted me to learn.

According to Dowlo, the purpose of education in Somalia is not different from the purpose of education in the U.S. In Somalia, "it was to become educated. To get rid of ignorance. For our parents, it was to do better than they did. To make advancement. To help our people and ourselves. To get better jobs." In the U.S., it is "not different. You send your child to school to prepare him for better future. To learn something. To be part of the world. Look at the homeless and the educated. Education is very important."

When it comes to the purpose of the Koranic education, she describes it as an obligation and tradition which must be done. "Allah requires from us. We have to teach them Allah's book and the way of life. This is the way we were taught. And we have to pass this to our children."

Dowlo believes that Somali community members have similar interests: to educate their children. She also acknowledges the diversity within the community. Like Idil and Jama, she considers herself more involved in schools than many Somali parents. "By Allah, We are all different. Yet, I believe we have the same interest and background. Those who are wise will see things the same way I see things.

We have to educate our children as long as we are in this world."

Dowlo believes that she is an involved parent. To her, an involved parent must attend parent-teacher conferences, help children with the homework, and monitor the grades of the children. Also, parents must talk to their children about education and schools.

> It is a big thing. It is important. To meet teachers; to help them with the homework; to be aware about his grade, and; encourage him by telling him the importance of education. And show him some examples of people who are successful and those who are not, and role of education in their situations. I give them the options. I ask them: do you want to be a lawyer or a housekeeper? They understand.

Dowlo elaborated on her involvement in her son's education in the following statement:

> I do a lot. I encourage him. I make him realize that he is a big boy. I teach him how to deal with his peers. I meet the teachers. I ask him to respect teachers. I require from him to pay attention during the class. I tell him how to stay out of trouble and change seats when

101

other students are giving him hard time. I ask him about his day while we are in the car. I ask him if there were any problems, or things he wants to share with me. I do not want him to forget. That is why I ask him in the car. My kids do not take the bus to schools. I transport them to the schools. I do not want them to get in trouble in the buses. I do not want them to get pushed and I do not want them to learn swearing and horsing. I find for them people who can help.

Dowlo is involved in her son's Koranic school more than she is involved in his public school. She believes the ability to communicate with the Koranic schoolteachers in Somali is the reason.

I am always there. I even talk to the teachers alone. I talk to them about how my kids learn. I also mediate when my children and the teachers have issues. I work on how to make the best environment for my children. I give ideas. We are on the same page. It is always different than the way I deal with schoolteachers. I trust the Dugsi/Koran teachers more. We speak the same language.

At the school, I cannot communicate well. I cannot express all I want to say in English. All other parents are the same.

Dowlo believes that teachers in the U.S. like to put kids in trouble by asking them to write an apology letter, and Somali parents do not understand the system. "They [Somalis] believe the teachers are always right. The teachers here ask kids to apologize. Say sorry. They ask the kids to write his apology in a paper. They want to put in his record. They want to put him in trouble. Somalis do not understand the implication of signing papers and saying sorry. It is admitting wrongdoing. You are a teacher. You understand." Dowlo believes that teachers and schools keep records of the infractions or wrongdoings of students even after they leave the school, and will share these records with law enforcement agencies. In Somalia, teacher and students interactions were not shared with other agencies unless a crime was committed.

She believes that there are barriers to her participation in her child's middle school. She also offers some suggestions to overcome these barriers. Although she is the least educated of all participants, Dowlo understands how better communication between parents and school is in the best interest of the students. She urges schools to understand the parents' perspective and to engage them.

Time is the biggest issue. Yes. There are things we would solve by having more communication. We would have understood each other. Sometimes they think that I have attitude. Maybe my language and expressions. They think I am an angry woman. We Somalis talk loud. Americans think we are fighting. Teachers believe that I am angry. Is that due to my language or they want to ignore me and do not want to face the big issues. I do not know. Whenever I talk they look down to me. That is why I communicate with teacher as minimum as possible. Unless it is important.

Because schools did not approach Dowlo, she thinks some teachers do not want to talk to her.

No, they do not understand me. They ignore me. I sometime wished all the teachers were Somalis. I would have communicated with teacher effectively. Somalis will not ignore me. Schools need to work on their mistake. The Somali community is being abused. They do not know their rights. The reality. At the elementary level, they look at the clothes of the children. They ask students about their

104

emotions. They want to put the parents in trouble. They do not know whether the parents can buy good clothes for the children. They refer parents to DHHS and child protection. Teachers and schools are against the poor people.

In the third interview, after quick member checking I asked Dowlo if she wanted to add anything. She offered the following statement in which she listed existing issues and proposed some ideas.

I want share with you that when they call us for meetings, they call us for the meetings which are not important. They call us pumpkin festival. That is the things they want me to be involved. Not the important ones. They do not call me for the important meetings. They do not want my ideas. I never go to budget meetings. I think it is important.

She continues and contrasts the people who understand the education system to those in her community. "The people who know the system get what they want because they are at the table. No one want help the poor. I believe there is lack of communication. We do not understand the system. I believe the schools must change their communication style."

She elaborates and gives examples to explain what she means by "understanding the system." She uses the special education system as an example of the lack of understanding. She, equally blames the parents and the schools.

> Many Somalis are told their children need to be tested. For many Somalis, that is shocking news. Instead of working with the school, they get defensive. It is opportunity for the child. He will get help, but Somalis refuse. They do not believe in special education. The schools also stereotype. They want to medicate all Somali children, which is wrong. There are misunderstandings.

Dowlo also talked about her community members' perceptions about the work of social workers who are in the schools. She believes that the social workers have other agendas - to implicate parents rather than helping them with their children.

> Even in the presence of the interpreters. I saw people who are scared when they hear the social worker wants to talk to your child.

Somalis believe they will lose their children if the social workers talk to them. They know the social workers do not have good intentions. They want find out the things parents are not doing right. They ask, "do your parents hit you?" Our people are lost in this land. No one is helping them. The kids will end up in the street or in jail. No one is helping us. The system is not accommodating. We have special needs. We lost many children. We are traumatized and scared.

She concludes by appealing to educators and authorities to improve their communication with the Somali parents. She demands the system to be more inclusive.

If our children get help they will become professors. It is better to meet parents. It is better to have better communication. Teachers can show their intention by better communication. They do not need to stereotype. They cannot ignore the white people. They need to get closer to us. We can achieve better by working together.

Dowlo requested that I share her ideas with other teachers and principals.

Rahma

Rahma was the first person to accept my invitation.
Initially, she thought I was collecting information to induce
change in the school system. After a long explanation, she
signed the consent forms and asked me to come another day.
Rahma and her son live in a two-bedroom apartment in a
housing complex in Portland. I interviewed Rahma in her
home. At my initial visit, Rahma's son seemed suspicious
about my visit. He was curious to know about my project. I
briefly explained my intentions to him. He asked his mother
to not share his issues with me. Rahma and her son discussed
with me about their options of high school and perceptions
they have about the three high schools in Portland. After 20
minutes of casual conversations, I was able to start
interviewing Rahma. Like all other participants, I used
Somali language for all interviews with her.

Rahma came to the United States in 1998. She is a
widow and mother of two. Her oldest daughter does not live
with her. As young girl, Rahma dreamed of becoming a
nurse. "My goal was to go to university and become a nurse.
A midwife. I could not get there. I could not achieve my
dream. I got married." Rahma cannot write or read English.
However, she feels comfortable speaking to her children's
teachers in English. She only asks for an interpreter when she

108

gets angry at the teachers. "When I am angry, as a parent I get angry, I demand for an interpreter. I know I cannot express myself in English in all settings. I demand. I feel I need an interpreter. Things are not easy when you do not speak English well."

Rahma graduated from secondary school in Somalia. At her school, the language of instruction was Somali. "I went to school in Somalia. I graduated from high school in Somalia. The language of instruction was Somali. We were learning everything in Somali language except one Arabic class in the Intermediate School, and one English class in the Secondary School. I loved Math when I was in school."

Rahma described how her parents were involved in her education and schools: "My parents were involved in my education. Without their participation I could not do anything. You need uniforms, books, and everything. Parents must buy everything for you. Other than that, they used to go to the school when we get in trouble or fail."

Rahma believes the purpose of education in Somalia is similar to the purpose of education in the U.S.: "I think, the purpose of education is the same: to learn. To become educated, and for better future. To become someone." However, she contrasted the role of the educators in Somalia and in the U.S.

But teachers were like parents. Children were accountable to teachers as they are accountable to their parents. Teachers in America are totally different than the teachers in Somalia in two ways: First, in Somalia you are scared of the teachers. If you do wrong or do not do your homework, teacher will put you in front of the class. The results of the exams were posted on the board. It is public. Everyone can see your results. In this country, no one knows your scores. Even when you have "F". Second, teachers treat the kids as their children.

Similarly, Rahma questions the policy of placing children in age appropriate class.

Schooling is different in here than it was in my home. I am not pleased with placing kids in higher grades when their academic performance is low. They tell us kids have 90s for grades, and we learn that they read below grade level. That is frustrating. What does 90 for a grade mean when he is below grade level? It is something we do not comprehend as Somalis.

110

Rahma thinks her community members share her beliefs about the purpose of education. In Somali tradition, parents expect their children to care for them when they older. Rahma highlighted this important cultural distinction.

> It is to become educated. In America they say "no child behind." My community shares with me those beliefs. We are very tiny community. We know each other. Every Somali can tell you that children learn to become good people. That means they will be able to help us when we need them most. When we get older. We need them to help themselves and their parents.

Rahma loves to be involved in her children's schools. She makes appointments with teachers when she becomes aware that her son is not doing well academically.

> I love to be part in my children's education. Only recently I became involved in children's education. It was when my daughter was in her eighth grade. I go to schools for events, I ask teachers about my children's situations. I even make appointments to meet the teachers. They tell me. I made a deal with them. If my son's grades are not good, I need to know that

within a week. Not more than a week. The end of the semester is too late for me to know.

Rahma talks to her child about education. She meets the teachers of her child, and, unlike any of the other participants, Rahma not only focused on academic aspects of her children but also volunteered at her child's middle school. "I meet teachers. I volunteer at the school when I have time. I help with the lunch. I told them that I am ready for them anytime. I filled out the volunteer forms at the beginning of the school year." Also, finding academic assistance for her child is one her top priorities. "I like to find for him a tutor to help him with academics. He goes to a tutor. He gets help with math and reading. I pay money."

However, she suspects that schools do not want her to become involved because communicating with language minority parents will require interpreters, and that will cost the district money. "I would like to let you know that some of our parents want to be part of the parent organization which helps the schools. We do not know how. I am not sure if the schools want people who do not speak English to come to school meetings. It will require from them to bring interpreters. Maybe they do not want us to be part of the parent organizations."

Rahma is an active member in her child's Koranic school. She said, "I do participate as much as I can. I do many things. I take my child to the Mosque. I clean the center. I plan events with other parents. We talk about how we can do better. We bring food and snacks for the children. We also like to do the same for the school. We do not know how."

Rahma believes that her middle school child does not want her to be involved in his school. She uses volunteering at his school as a discipline tool to correct his motivational and behavioral issues.

He has motivation issues. He gets in trouble. Middle school is different than elementary school. When kids are in elementary schools do not mind when their parents come to the school. Middle school children do not want you to come to the school at all. For example, I volunteered at the school. And my child does not want me to volunteer. He does not want to see me at the cafeteria. I told him that I will leave when his class is coming for lunch. I leave the Cafe when his class is coming for lunch. I told him if his grade is good, I will transfer to another place. To the Library. It

113

worked for me. He started doing his homework.

Rahma thinks that teachers want her to participate. "They always say come and participate." However, she accuses one of the administrators in her son's school of misrepresenting facts and wanting to get her son in trouble.

> Things were good. The assistant principal was not good. My son is a teenager. But the assistant principal picks on him. The assistant principal even mischaracterizes my son to implicate him. The social worker took the case. She is much better than the assistant principal. She works with us very well. She even put my son in an anger management program. She knows how to help. She understands him.

Rahma wished me good luck, and asked me to not share her identity with her son's teachers and assistant principal.

Idil

I knew Idil more than anyone of the other interviewees. She accepted my invitation to be interviewed without hesitation. She lives in public housing complex in Portland, Maine. All four of her children go to Portland

114

Public Schools. However, the busy single mother gave short answers to most of my questions. It seemed to me that she wanted to be done with interviews. I interviewed the young single mother of four in her house. She is a busy mother. Before I started the interview, she asked me permission if it was fine to continue fixing her daughter's hair. I had to stop the interviews and recording several times because she was attending to her children's needs. At the beginning of my first interview Idil's daughter shared fruits with me.

Before her arrival in the U.S Idil lived in the Indian Subcontinent with her mother and siblings as refugees for years. Her father died in Somalia. She finished high school in Pakistan and she speaks English well. "I speak English well. Not as a native. I am ok. I studied English in Pakistan. I did not go school in the U.S."

Idil's parents were involved in her education. "Yes. They were involved. They enrolled me and my siblings in schools. They bought for us books and notebooks. They found someone who was helping us with homework. They were very involved. Not the American way. We did not need them to come to the school. We behaved well. Involvement in children's education does not mean to be at the school and doing the teachers' jobs."

Idil thinks that the purpose of education is the same all over the world: "To establish better future. I think the purpose of education is the same everywhere. I tell my kids that education is the key for better future. Without education, one will become homeless in the U.S. Kids must do well in schools to do well in this world."

Like Jama, Idil believes as Muslims, Somalis must send their children to Koranic schools. "We are Muslims. We have to send our kids to schools for better future in this world. The Koranic school is for hereafter. It is moral obligation. We are ordered by Allah to teach our kids about their religion while they are young. Allah will not ask you about why you did not send your children to public school. However, you will be asked about their religious education."

Idil acknowledges the diversity in her community and how they are learning about the U.S. education system in different ways. "My community members are very diverse. The common thing is that we are all learning about U.S. system of education. Everything about the U.S. is new to us." She goes on and describes members of her community as uneducated and accuses them of allowing their children to do things that are not permitted in Islam. "There are some Somali women who do not care. They are not educated. They do not care about the kids. They allow their kids to do things, which are not allowed in Islam. They do not tell their children about the importance of education. That is why we have so many boys in jail." She elaborated her statement further after I probed her to say more about her statement.

> Are you asking me what makes them neglect their children? The fingers are not the same. Humans are different. You see every day some Americans who are losers. We as Somalis will have also losers. Unless we go back to our culture, we will have many losers. I have many women who are acting as young girls. How they can take care of children. They need help. They need to be educated. I believe.

I asked her about what she means by "education." She responded, "I do not know. How to take care for their children?"

Idil considers herself a very involved mother. She supports her middle school child's learning in many ways.

> I buy what they need for their schools. I am aware that I am not very rich. But I try to provide what they need. I give my daughter ride to school. I do not want her to take the school bus. There are many trouble-making children who take the bus. Bad influence. I

pay for tutor. I pay $100 per month for two hours a week. I attend the parent-teacher conferences. I advise my kids. I want every one of children to be someone. I want them to become medical doctors. Insha Allah (God willing).

She considers time and childcare the biggest obstacles to her involvement in the schools of her children. "Time is always is an issue. For me childcare is the biggest issue. I have three other kids. I cannot leave them in the house. I have to ask/beg my neighbors to watch my kids while I attend conferences."

According to Idil, "Middle schools are different than the elementary schools. Both teachers and our own children do not want us to be at the school. In the past they call us to come and join them for field trips and school events. Now, no communication. And my daughter, understandably does not want me to be at the school. She is young. So the middle school is different."

Idil refused to answer whether educators and school administrators want her to participate in the schools of her children. "I cannot say anything about that. Maybe," she said. She also believes that teachers who do not know her daughter treat her as an English Language Learner, even though her daughter is an English speaker and smart. "When the teachers are new or at the start of the school, some teachers think about my daughter she is new to the country. They treat her like ESL. She is born here, and she is smart girl. It takes them little time to realize that. I also tell the teachers at the beginning of the year about my kids."

Idil worries about the future of her children. "I am scared. I do not want my kids uneducated. I want them to be smart and to become wealthy. I am scared whenever I hear a Somali child is arrested or had car accident. Or could not finish his school on time. I mean cannot graduate. It is scary environment. I only ask Allah to watch my kids."

She concluded her interview with two wishes. "I wish the educated people like you to tell us about their experiences," and "I wish they separated the bad kids from the good one. The bad kids always influence the good ones. In America they will keep everyone in the same place. That is why I do not send my kids with the bus. Nothing else."

At the end of my last interview, Idil wished me good luck, and promised me that she will be there for me if I need to interview her again.

Jama

I met Jama in his house. He is a practicing conservative Muslim. During our interview he was reminding

119

his children about prayer times. The house was not a typical Somali house with four children. Often, Somali children are active and play or speak loud. The children were very respectful, and seemed mature for their ages. Jama's wife did not come out to the living room when I was there. Meeting the opposite gender and socializing is prohibited in conservative Islamic teaching interpretations. I believe that is why Jama's wife did not greet me. Like Rahma and Dowlo, he wanted me to initiate change in schools through my writing.

Jama has an undergraduate degree in Islamic Law from a prestigious university in a Middle Eastern country. He came to the United States as a refugee in 1999. He lives with his wife and four children in a housing project in Portland. Jama moved from the South to Maine eight years ago. Currently, he drives a Taxi in Portland. His four children were born in the U.S. They all go to Portland Public Schools.

Jama, proudly summarized his educational experiences in the following statement:

> I started my education in a "Dugsi" (Koranic school). I learned the Koran. I mean, I memorized the entire 114 chapters. I did not go to primary school. I started at the middle school in Mogadishu, Somalia. They tested me

in Arabic, Koran, and Math. Then I was
admitted at the middle school level. The
school was affiliated with Al-Azhar. Then,
went to high school. It was in Arabic also.
Then I got scholarship to go to Egypt for
university. To Al-Azhar University. I started
learning Sharia law in Al-Azhar. After, I
completed my study, I got the chance to come
to America.

Jama went to an Adult Education school in Texas for
a few months. He speaks enough English to communicate
with his children's teachers. He does not ask for an
interpreter when he is meeting the teachers. He believes that
the interpreters do not know English better than he does. He
feels comfortable speaking to the teachers.

I do not speak English as a native. I have
moments when I do not understand the
conversations. I do not ask for facilitator. I
know the facilitators also are like my level. I
talk to the teachers. They are welcoming. The
teachers in America work as business people.
They welcome you as they want to sell
something to you. In Somalia, you know, they
will tell you that your child did this and that.

In the U.S., teachers will tell you good news before they tell you about the bad news. In Somalia, the only news you hear is the bad one.

While in middle and high school, Jama did not live with his parents. "My father died after he placed me at Koranic school. I was five years old. Then my mother supported me until I finished the Koran. She took care of me. But when I went to middle school and after, no one helped me. I did not live with my family. I was on my own. My mother lived in Ethiopia, and I lived in Somalia." Jama is originally from the Somali region of Ethiopia. He left Ethiopia to Somalia due to bloody war between Somalia and Ethiopia with territorial dispute in 1977.

Jama believes the purpose of schooling in both the U.S. and Somalia is the same: to get jobs. However, he states that Somalis send their children to schools for another purposes as well: to please Allah. "Like in Somalia, getting educated to get good job, and have a future. To live in comfortable life. It is like Somalia. In Somalia though, people educate themselves for the sake of Allah. For the sake of Allah, and to get rewards in hereafter."

To Jama, all Somalis must teach their children about their religion. "I am a Somali, and Somalis are Muslims. It is to learn the Koran and their religion. To be good Muslims. The Koran teacher is teaching them how to worship their Lord."

According to Jama, Somali community members share his idea about the purpose of education. "Yes, they share with me. We are poor people, and we want our children to do well. I do not want my children to be poor as well. They are smart." However, he believes that the biggest obstacle Somali community members face when they want to help their children in their education is lack of understanding of the U.S. education system. He believes in order to involve parents in the schools of their children, they must be educated first.

> In our community, the parents seem to me that they do not understand the reality. They did not get how the system in the U.S. is different than the system they experienced. There is a big difference. I can say 99% of my people do not understand how to educate children in here. Only few who are educated can understand. I mean educated in the U.S. The person should know the how. How the system works. Then that time, he can help the children. But when the parent does not know

the system, and how it works, then to help the children becomes difficult if not impossible.

Jama considers himself an involved father. For Jama, parental involvement means coming to the school whenever he is invited or called. He attends parent-teacher conferences and meets teachers whenever they call him. He reminds and sometimes helps his children with homework, and finds for them academic assistance when he cannot help them with their homework. He "even went one night to the budget meeting of the School Board."

> It seems to me two ways. To communicate with the schools, teachers, and to become aware about what is going on in the school. The other one is to work with the children at home. Helping them with the homework. I help my children with the homework. Sometimes I cannot help them. I do not know the content or the subject. I find for them someone who can help them most of the time. I remind them their homework all the time. I emphasize that. It is not necessary for the parents to know everything. But reminding them to do their homework is important. I go

to meetings. Whenever teachers call me. I ask them about my kids.

Jama appeals to educators and schools to work with Somali parents effectively. He wants educators to tell the parents about their expectations. Jama expressed his willingness to learn about the U.S. system of education and work with educators and schools in educating his children. He believes that the voices of Somali parents are not heard, and their absence from the table affects their children's education negatively.

> I do not have anything else to add to what I told you. I only wish schools will educate us about the education system in the U.S. Many of us do not understand the system. We are a big part of the community. They must consider us as partners. I mean like they do with the white people. Schools are for all. Somalis are in Portland for long time. It is close to 20 years. We do not see any change in the state of education of our children. Our children perform below grade level. School must work with us to break this cycle. We did not come to the U.S. to be at bottom of the social class forever.

125

Jama's interaction with his child's school is influenced by his experience in Somalia. He does not go to the schools of his children without calls or invitations from the teachers. He likes to give the teachers and children the time. "I go to the schools whenever I am called. I do not know what to do at the school if I go. It is also good to give the teachers the time to spend with children. I do not want to spend their time and my time with no reason. If my son is not doing well, I expect the teachers to call me. And of course, I will leave my workplace to address the issue. Otherwise, I am not going there."

Jama does not have previous experience in raising middle school children in the U.S. However, what he is hearing from Somali community members scares him. "I do not have enough experiences with middle school children. I have my oldest one at the middle school. People talk about middle school as the place where children learn about drugs and sex, and all the bad things. So far, my son is doing well. I think. I hope the younger ones will do the same."

At the end of my third interview, Jama asked me to keep him informed about my progress, and provide him a copy of my dissertation.

Farah

Farah accepted to be interviewed for the study easily. Because of his educational background, he easily understood my reasons for conducting this research. He invited me into his house. I interviewed him three times in his house. His wife and children were welcoming. They served tea and Somali sweets during the interviews. Each time, after short conversation and check-ins, I proceeded to ask my interview questions.

Farah was born in Somalia. He came to the United States in 1996 with his wife and three children. Now, Farah is the father of eight children. The oldest two attend local university, and the youngest goes to pre-school. Five of his eight children were born in the U.S. All 10 family members share a four bedroom apartment with a tiny living room. Farah came to the U.S. under the U.S. Lottery Visa Program. Currently, Farah works 12-hour night shifts for four days a week. Farah's wife stays home and takes care of the children

Farah finished four years of college in Somalia. His degree was in Arabic language and journalism. He does not speak English fluently and did not go to school to learn English in the U.S. At the parent-teacher conferences, Farah and his wife do not ask for an interpreter. They can communicate with teachers in English. He is busy with work

127

and raising children. "I do not speak English as I do in Somali. I learned English when I was in Somalia. I did not acquire more in the U.S. I am a father. I am busy with the children. It is not about me anymore. I have to take care of them. I went to University in Somalia. We studied English as a subject. One period or may be two a week."

Farah believes in education and wants his children to do well in school. He believes one should be educated to get a better life. "When you are educated you will be in better situation than others who are not educated. Education makes you someone. I want my children to get good education and get good jobs as outcomes." He believes the purpose of education in both Somalia and the U.S. is the same. "People in the entire world seek education for better tomorrow."

Farah's father was educated, and involved in his children's education. However, both of Farah's parents passed away while he was in high school. "Both of my parents died in my high school years. They were involved. My father was educated. He used to help me with the homework. He hired tutors for us. My father loved education. He wanted me to be someone. Whenever I get good grades, my father used to buy me new clothes or shoes. I was getting rewards. He loved math. He wanted me to learn math."

Farah contrasted schooling in America and in Somalia.

> My schooling was totally different than schooling in the U.S. Or maybe I am wrong. I did not experience schooling in the U.S. I am feeling that my children or the children in the U.S. have more opportunities. We did not have books to read. We did not have libraries. We were poor. The entire country was poor. Teachers were friendly. However, students were serious. We were competing to be the best. Our parents were not coming to schools. No parent-teacher conferences. Pupils and educators solved all learning issues. Our parents provided us food and clothes. I wished that was the case in the U.S. I am tired of doing everything.

Farah believes that Somali community members care about the education of their children, "My community shares this understanding: the love of education." However, he contends that American educators do not understand what the Somali parents expect from them. For example, Somali parents believe that what happens in the school is between the teacher and the student. Here that is not the case. "My community members have different traditions. They trust the educators/teachers and schools. Teachers in America do not consider themselves more than teachers. They only teach. They cannot compel pupils to pay attention and learn. Parents can do that." He also blames Somali parents for their lack of understanding of the American school systems.

Many of them their bodies are here, and their heads are in Somalia or Africa. They deal with schools and children similar to when they were in Somalia. So, they think the teachers in the U.S. are similar to the teachers they had when they were students in Somalia. They are wrong. Here the system is different. I learned about the difference very quickly.

As far as Farah's involvement in his children's schools is concerned, he only goes to schools for parent-teacher conferences, graduations, and when his children get into trouble.

To me, involvement does not mean going to the school almost every week. I am sure teachers will not like you if you are at the school every day. Children do not like that as well. Sometimes I go, or maybe my wife goes to the school open-house. We always go when the children are starting a new school. We both went to the graduations of our older children. My wife goes 90% of the time. I work at the night time. We also go to the school whenever one of our kids gets in trouble. I have five boys. You can imagine how boys can get in trouble easily.

He wants educators to know that parents are busy working and taking care of younger children. A typical Somali family consists of more than five children, and that makes it difficult for parents to go to schools with young children. Additionally, most Somalis work as blue-color employees. They may work second and third shifts. Farah believes that he is involved to his understanding and capacity.

I do well now. I am sure it is not enough in schools. I cannot do what the white people do. Even my children do not want me to go the school every time. And I have to work. Lawyers and rich people can go to schools. Not me! I work at nights. As I said before, I try to help them with the homework. The older ones, who go to the University of Southern Maine help the younger ones.

131

At home, he or his older children help the younger children with school and Koran homework. "As I said, I go to every parent-teacher conference. I help them with the homework. I am not good at math. Geometry and Algebra. Their older siblings who are in college always help them. I am involved." He also advises his children. He says "I talk to them about the importance of education."

Farah wants schools to provide safe places for students to do their homework. He expresses safety and economic concerns. Schools must provide the children a safe environment. Other participants also shared similar concerns about community centers. Somali parents are very protective and fear of losing their children to drugs and jails is widespread in the community.

> They [the schools] need to provide after
> school program with teachers. I do not want to
> send my children to the community centers.
> There are drug dealers and bad people in the
> neighborhood. Schools should establish their
> own homework or after school programs. I
> bought a printer for my children. I did not
> have money. I borrowed the money from a
> friend. I know many people cannot afford
> printers and internet, and kids will tell the

132

parents to go to the libraries. They will meet bad people on their way. So many Somali kids are in jail.

When I asked Farah whether he shared his suggestions with educators, he expressed powerlessness.

Who am I? Who am I to tell them what to do? I am sure they know what they are doing. I know they will say no money for these programs. It is beyond what I can understand. The people who work for the government. They make the decisions. I am only worried for my kids. I do not want them to meet bad influence in community centers. I live in a housing project. I ask Allah to protect my children.

He also suggests changes in the content children are learning in schools. "The kids in America do not know about the world very well. They read stories which are not true (fiction). I want them to read what is going on in the world. I want them to read history and learn geography. I want them to learn about current events."

Farah believes that middle school age children are more challenging than elementary and high school children. He acknowledges developmental and cultural challenges he faces when he is dealing with his young teenagers. "They think they are smart and old enough to manage their own affairs. It is not easy, and the older they get it will not get easier. We, Somalis have conservative community values. We like to make decisions for our children. Even, regarding marriage. It is difficult in the US. Children are free from family influences."

Farah feels pressure from his wife to participate more in their children's education. "My wife compares me to the other men who are very involved in the education of their children." At that moment, his wife was not in the room with us. He also feels guilt and acknowledges short-comings. "I also envy other Somalis who have the time to spend with their children."

At the end of my third interview, Farah and his older children told me that they were happy to see a Somali person who is going to graduate school, and they wished me good luck with my research.

Summary of the Interviews

In the second phase of the study, I interviewed five parents of middle school children. The participants were members of the initial pool of subjects who responded to the survey. The interviews provided more depth to the survey responses by elaborating on the backgrounds of the Somali parents who participated in the study, their experiences of schooling, their beliefs about education, and their engagement in their children's schools. I collected demographic data of the participants and their educational experiences in Somalia and elsewhere. I also recorded participants' experiences as parents with the U.S. education systems, their perception about education and schools, and their views on their involvement in their children's education and schools. I used Seidman's (2006) interviewing steps to collect the qualitative data. The order of the presentation of the qualitative data was based on the degree of satisfaction of the parent with their children's schools.

Observations Regarding the Participants

I looked at the demographics of the participants in relation to their parental involvement very closely. I observed that the two male participants were least involved in the schools of their children. At the same time, they indicated the most satisfaction. Farah admits that his wife is more involved in their children's schools. Additionally, he directs his older children to help the younger ones, while Jama puts more responsibility on his son. He asks him to seek help from the teachers when he needs help.

Educational attainment of the parents is another demographic factor that might influence parents' intentions and their behaviors regarding school involvement. Even though all participants acknowledged the lack of knowledge of the American educational system as a drawback, the data show that the most educated participants are the least involved. Both Jama and Farah are males and hold university degrees, and they are the least involved in the schools of their children and relatively comfortable with the education system.

Dowlo and Rahma are the least educated of the five participants. Yet, they are most involved in their children's schools. Although they expressed the greatest dissatisfaction with the schools of their children, they monitor their children's grades and performance in the classroom before their children fail classes. They understand the grading system, and use email or visit the school when their child is not performing well in the class. The two women accuse the school system, and to some extent the teachers, with systematic exclusion. They both talk about how their boys were mistreated by teachers and administrators. However, I observed that they are the only two out of the five parents who reported their children got in trouble in the schools. It is their relatively enhanced school involvement is correlated to their children's behavior in the schools.

I placed Idil in the middle of the dissatisfaction continuum. Idil is the youngest of all participants and speaks English well. She went to high school in English in Asia. She attends parent-teacher conferences and reminds teachers about her daughter's good academic standing. She does not want her daughter to be perceived as an ELL student.

Application of TPB

In the next sections, I will present the actual behaviors and intentions of the interviews, followed by behavioral beliefs, norms, and controls that influence the intentions and the behaviors.

Behaviors and Intentions. All participants said they see that their involvement in their children's school is a positive factor that can influence the schooling process of their children. Participants acknowledge that they need to do better and hope to improve their parental involvement in their children's public schools. However, despite their willingness to be involved more, they believe that their intentions cannot be materialized as behaviors without knowing the U.S. education system. Lack of time was another factor that influenced their intentions. A majority of the participants said they believe they would have been more involved in their children's schools if they had the time.

137

Despite their beliefs and perceptions about other relevant groups such as educators, their own children, and other controlling factors, Somali parents perceive themselves as involved parents and willing to work with educators and schools. To them, parental involvement means going to school events only when invited. Ironically, they are aware that their understanding was not correct, and they recognize that they need to change their previous way of dealing with schools. However, all five participants said that they did not know how to get involved in the public schools. Only Rahma said she volunteered at her child's school.

In contrast to their engagement with public schools, all participants said they are involved in their children's religious schools. They said they volunteer at the religious schools and continuously communicate with the teachers at the religious schools. Even though religious education is a part of the Somali culture, parents' involvement in the religious schools of their children is a sign that the study participants have intentions to be involved in their children's schools, but they do not understand the public education the same way they understand the *Dugsi* system.

Beliefs. All participants indicate that education was every important. They believe that their children can financially do well in their new country only by acquiring good education.

When I asked participants about the purpose of education, their responses were closely aligned: to do well financially and socially. They also mentioned that their parents and other members of their community shared their beliefs regarding the purpose of education. Nevertheless, they drew a line between religious and public education (schooling). They believe religious education helps children to develop good character while schooling helps them to achieve financial gains.

All Somali parents who were interviewed acknowledged that their experiences in U.S. public schools were different from their previous experience of schools in Somalia and elsewhere, noting that in Somalia, teachers are more like parents of the children, so the teachers discipline them and care about them in the way that parents do. In the US, they have learned that the teachers are not expected to act like parents, so they understand that they are expected to be involved as parents. They also shared their ideas regarding what kids are learning and the role of the parents.

Normative Influences. These participants' perceptions about the expectations of others influence their intentions and behaviors regarding their parental involvement are very important factors in this investigation. These include Somali community members, their own middle school children, and the educators. Jama, Farah, and Idil expressed general feelings about the lack of communication and connection with schools. While Dowlo and Rahma, who expressed the least satisfaction with the schools of their children, suspect the reason for the lack of communication between the language minority parents and the schools of their children is a way in which schools deliberately exclude minority parents in the education process. They expressed the belief that schools do not want to include them in the schooling process because of their status as language minority group. Additionally, both Rahma and Dowlo talked about their negative interactions with schools and shared specific complaints. Dowlo contrasted elementary and middle schools. She observed that teachers at the elementary level were willing to engage parents more than the middle school teachers.

Additionally, while they said they believe Somali community members expect them to be involved in their children's schools, they believe that their own middle school children do not want them to be involved in their schools. Rahma, Jama, and Idil are sure that their own middle school children do not want them to come to the school. Rahma understands her son's dislike and threatens him that she will volunteer at the school if his grades are not good. She

140

indicates her belief that this type of parental involvement as a way to mitigate her son's lack of motivation and work completion.

Perceived Behavioral Controls. As I mentioned above, Somali parents who participated in this study say they believe that they are not included in ways that other mainstream parents are included. Additionally, the participants of the investigation told me they believe their limited ability to speak English, lack of or poor communication with schools, lack of time, type of their employment, and child care commitment were other factors which limit their involvement in their children's schools. Furthermore, four of the five participants expressed general safety concerns for their children. They mentioned that many Somali children drop out of schools and some are in prisons. Farah, Rahma, and Idil considered their neighborhoods dangerous and expressed safety concerns. They did not allow their children to access a neighborhood-learning center out of fear for their children's safety. Idil and Dowlo did not send their children on school buses because they do not want them to be in the same place with the "bad children." Having presented the data of the study, in the next chapter, I will look at the theory to help us understand how behaviors and intentions of Somali parents

who participated in the study are influenced by their
behavioral, normative, and control beliefs.

CHAPTER FIVE

ANALYSIS

As I stated in previous chapters, the purpose of this research was to explore perceptions of the parents of Somali children who are in Portland Public Schools regarding education and schooling of their children and the perceptions, intentions, and behavior of these parents regarding their involvement in their children's education and schooling. In Chapter Four, the data from the survey and from interviews were presented. The purpose of this chapter is to share the results from the analysis of the survey and the interviews in order to address the research questions. The chapter starts with listing the research questions followed by a description of the analytic process, the results of the data analysis, and presentation of the results. I relied on Ajzen's Theory of Planned Behavior (TPB) to analyze data and to organize the presentations of the results. TPB relates individual's intentions and actual behaviors to his/her beliefs, willingness to meet the expectation of his/her social circles, and his/her perceptions of behavioral controls. The chapter ends with a presentation of the major findings of the investigation.

This study was guided by three broad research questions concerning the perceptions of Somali parents about education and schooling and their involvement in their children's education and schools. The first two questions are:

1) How do first generation Somali parents of middle school students, who are part of a refugee population settled in Portland, Maine view education and schooling?

2) How are first generation Somali parents, who are part of a refugee population settled in Portland, Maine, involved in their middle school children's education in general, schooling in particular, and what factors influence their involvement?

I did not collect data related to research question three. Research question three states: What are the perceptions of Somali parents of middle school students who are part of a refugee population settled in Portland, Maine whose children are or have been part of English Language Learners (ELL) programs with regard to the expectations of their children and the responsibilities of parents in the school?

144

As I mentioned in chapter three, in the process of collecting data, I realized that parents with children in the ELL programs were not included in the sample I selected for the interviews. All interviewees reported that their children were born in the U.S. and had never been part of the ELL programs. However, data addressing aspects of my third research question, such as Somali parents' perceptions with regard to their expectations of their children and their responsibilities as parents, are embedded in the data collected with regard to research questions one and two.

Analytical Process

To analyze the survey data, I followed quantitative method traditions. Tables and charts were used to present the data. The charts showed a simplified version of participants' responses to the survey questions in the form of percentages and numbers. I used tables to depict participants' profiles and to list categories and subcategories that emerged from the study.

My initial engagement with interview data was inductive. I used a dynamic process in which field notes and participants' narratives were used to create initial codes. Additionally, I used the research questions and the Theory of Planned Behavior (TPB) as a framework for analyzing the data deductively. I found TPB very suitable for analyzing the

145

data I collected. The theory has a framework which links a person's beliefs, social norms, and perceived behavioral controls to individual's intentions and actions.

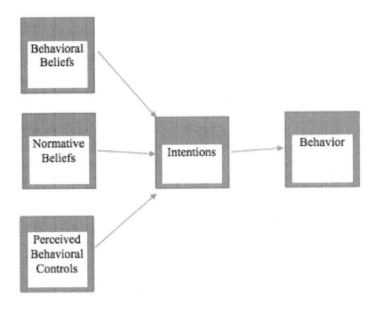

Figure 5.1. Constructs of TPB (Ajzen, 1991).

Additionally, I present the coded categories and subcategories in table 5.1. I used participants' own words and percentages of survey responses, where applicable in the narrative as evidence to support the categories and to focus my analysis. After examining the initially coded categories and using TPB as theoretical background for my analysis, I categorized the data into these four categories: Beliefs about behaviors in question (the actions or reactions of a person in

146

response to external or internal stimuli); normative beliefs (a combination of perceived expectations from relevant individuals or groups along with the intentions to comply with these social expectations); perceived behavioral controls (perception about the ease or the difficulty of performing a behavior) for families regarding their parental involvement; and intentions and behaviors which, are according to the theory, results of the beliefs, subjective norms, and behavioral controls.

Table 5.1. Coded Categories and Subcategories According to TPB

TPB CATEGORIES	Subcategories
Behavioral Beliefs (Somali parents' beliefs about education, schooling and parental involvement.)	Purpose and importance of education (Public and Religious)
Normative Beliefs (Somali parents' perceived expectations from educators, schools, community, and their own middle school children, their intentions to comply with these expectations.)	Somali Community norms and expectations, organizational expectations, religious and public school teachers' expectation Children's expectation
Perceived Behavioral Controls (Somali parents' perceived ease or difficulty in participating in their children's education and schooling.)	Institutional opportunities and barriers Ability to speak English Type of employment and amount of time available Child care issues Lack of communication from schools
Intention (Intentions of Somali parents to participate in children's schooling).	Hope to be involved .

Behavior (The actions or reactions of Somali parents regarding their involvement in their children's education and schooling)	Parent-teacher conference Homework and academic assistance Waiting invitation from the teachers Monitoring children's grades Non-academic activities

Somali Parents' Beliefs about Purpose and Importance of Education

According to Ajzen's Theory of Planned Behavior, a belief is a very important factor in individuals' developing intentions to perform (or not to perform) a specific behavior/action. In this study, Somali parents' beliefs about the importance and the purpose of education influence their intentions and the subsequent behavior towards their participation in their children's education and schooling. It is important to understand how demographic factors of the participants might influence their views on education and schooling. In this sub section, I present how Somali parents described their views of education and schooling with specific examples regarding their views and show how these views/beliefs inform their intentions and behavior to be involved in their children's public and religious schools.

149

Parents' Beliefs about the Purpose of Public Schooling

In the context of this research, education is a broad term that encompasses secular and religious education. For the purpose of this study, "education" is defined as the act of preparing children intellectually for a productive life. Education encompasses many aspects of the educative process of children including public and religious schooling, while schooling is the institutionalization of education in grades and with a set curriculum. However, almost all of the participants described education and public schools as having the same meaning and as interchangeable. So, I had to clarify for participants the difference between the two based on my operational definitions of the two words. In contrast, parents were clear about the definition of religious education because religious education is part of the Somali culture.

Nevertheless, all survey respondents and interviewees said religious and public education of their children were equally very important and expressed intentions to participate in their children's religious and public education and schools. Somali parents view education and sending children to school not only as a means to a brighter future and better financial gains but also as a religious obligation. All participants asserted with confidence that the purpose of education is the

150

same all over world: to prepare children for a better future. They cited financial gain as the single most important factor that motivates them to support their children in public schools. Some lamented that their economic status would have been better if they were educated, and they expressed their intention to break the cycle of poverty by educating the next generation. Jama said, "We are poor people, and we want our children to do well. I do not want my children to be poor as well." Idil remarked "I want them to be smart and to become wealthy."

Somali parents who participated in the study expressed that they want to do whatever it takes to educate their children. Some participants proudly mentioned how they coupled their beliefs and intentions to prepare their children for upward mobility with actions/behavior. Rahma and Idil hired tutors to help their children with their homework. Idil said "I pay $100 for each child every month. Their education is important to me." While Farah, despite his meager resources said, "I borrowed money from a friend and bought a printer for my children." Clearly, some Somali parents prioritize educational costs in the family budget.

Participants' shared with me their views on curriculum, role of the teacher and the school, and their responsibilities as parents. They were qualifying their views on these school related issues by referencing their schooling experiences in Somalia.

Curriculum and Class Management. Very few Somali parents of middle school children who participated in the study expressed dissatisfaction with the content that their children are learning. Farah (who was educated in Somalia) put forward some curriculum related suggestions. He proposed that children be taught core academic subjects and learn about current events. "I want them to read what is going on in the world. I want them to read history and learn geography. I want them to learn about current events." And for children to behave well, they should be punished and rewarded.

Role of the Educator and the School. Historically, in Somalia, schools and teachers made all school related decisions, and parents did not have any input in the schooling process. Parents were not involved in school issues. Understandably, all participants in the study reported that they do not like getting calls about their children from the schools. Jama spoke for all Somalis and used "we". He said, "We [Somalis] do not like to come to schools." They want all school related matters to be between the teacher and the students. Farah said, "Pupils and educators solved all learning issues. Our parents provided us food and clothes only. I wish that was the case in the U. S. I am tired of doing everything."

By everything he meant tracking his child's grades, ensuring homework was complete, attending parent-teacher conferences, and getting academic assistance for him.

Furthermore, these parents indicate that they believe that most of these calls are prompted by their children getting into trouble. Farah said "I do not like to be called. I think something went wrong." They are aware of the notion of bringing parents to schools as a corrective behavioral measure for the children. This is a common practice in U.S. schools and potentially makes all parents anticipate bad news whenever they receive phone communication from their children's schools.

Nevertheless, the participants realize how the teacher's role in Somalia is different from the educator's role in the United States. The influence of their experience is evident in their conclusions. They believe that the teachers they experienced were better than their children's teachers in the U.S. They repeatedly mentioned that teachers in Somalia were like parents; they advised and considered their students as their children. In contrast, participants observed that in the U.S teachers teach only academic subjects and do not deal with students as Somali teachers did. Some participants expressed that they preferred the Somali way, and all of them say they believe their children will learn better if the teachers adopt the Somali way. This is a major factor in why parental involvement of Somali parents is problematic.

Responsibilities of Parents. The data from the interviews show that Somali parents respect the teachers of their children and school authorities in general. Respect for authority in a hierarchical structure is an important aspect in the Somali culture and is inherent in their religion. In Islam, teachers are regarded as parents and, as practicing Muslims, all interviewees indicated that they adhere to Islamic teachings. Religious teachers receive more respect than public education teachers. All participants believe going to the school without an invitation from the teacher shows disrespect to the educator, and they are certain that educators will disapprove of such behavior. Farah said, "I am sure teachers will not like you if you are at the school every day." This perception of the need for an invitation to participate influences the attitude of Somali parents towards their children's schools. However, participants seemed to understand the culture in their new environment is different from their culture and wish to try to navigate the system. For example, Dowlo questioned the intentions of her son's teachers when her son was accused of something that he did not do. Similarly, Rahma described one of the administrators as unfair and as someone who wanted to get her son in trouble. Such encounters with educators and school administrators are foreign in Somali culture.

Parents' Beliefs about the Purpose of Religious Schooling

Almost all school age Somali children attend after school and/or weekend religious schools. Somalis call the religious school "*dugsi*." In North America, *dugsi* is held in mosques. At the *dusgi*, children memorize the Koran and learn Islamic manners. Among Muslims worldwide, Somalis are known for memorizing the Koran. The majority of the teachers at the *dugsi* are from the Somali community. They charge nominal fees that most community members can afford. *Dugsi* teachers are highly regarded and respected by both the students and teachers. Because parents speak the same language as the *dugsi* teachers, they communicate with the teachers effectively. Dowlo highlights the importance of trust between teachers and families and language. She said "I give ideas. We are on the same page. It is always different than the way I deal with public school teachers. I trust the *Dugsi*/Koran teachers more. We speak the same language. At the school, I cannot communicate well. I cannot express all I want to say in English. All other parents are the same."

When it comes to the purpose of religious education, all survey respondents and interview participants said that

155

religious education is very important for their children. The interviewees reported that they provide religious education for their children for moral and spiritual reasons. Idil said "We are ordered by Allah to teach our kids about their religion while they are young." In addition to responding to Allah's call, they want their children to gain the Islamic knowledge and learn values to become good people. In other words, they view religious education and public education as complementary processes. They believe attending religious and public schools are important for the overall wellbeing of the child. Rahma explained, "It [purpose of education] is to be educated and acquire good manners."

In general, Somali parents of middle school children who participated in this investigation believe that both public and religious education are essential for their children. The two main reasons for educating their children are to help them become good individuals and gain wealth. They also indicated that they view schooling in certain ways which are different from the ways the educators view it.

I have presented the results of my investigation about Somali parents' beliefs about education and schooling. Next, I will present the behavioral norms that affect Somali parents and will explain how social norms and expectations of relevant groups such as community members, their children, and educators, influence parents' intentions toward and interactions with their children's schools.

Behavioral Norms and their Effects on Somali Parents' Intentions and Behavior

According to TPB, community and social norms influence individual's intentions and behavior to comply with the expectations of relevant groups. For this study, behavioral/subjective norms are the perceived expectations of Somali parents from relevant groups and individuals regarding their parental involvement in their children's schools. The data from the survey and the interviews show the common expectations that influence Somali parents' intentions and behavior towards parental involvement. These expectations are from the following relevant groups: a) Somali community norms and expectations, b) the school's organizational expectations, c) public school teachers' expectations, c) religious school teachers' expectation and, e) their children's expectations. In other words, they recognize the normative expectations in their own community and in the larger population of the city as well as the members of the public school community

Somali Community Members' Expectations

Somali parents who responded to the survey and participated in the interviews expressed their loyalty to their

Somali community. Occasionally, they mentioned diversity within the Somalis in Portland, yet they described the community as united when it comes to the purpose and importance of education, schooling, and parental involvement. They used phrases such as, "we are very small community," "everyone knows everyone," and "my community shares this understanding: the love of education."

Sixty-five percent of the survey respondents said that their community members expect them to be involved in their children's education. Similarly, all interviewees reported that their community members expect them to participate in their children's schools. Some participants said that some community members failed in regard to the community expectations because they are not involved in their children's education. Idil described them as "careless and uneducated" parents. Surprisingly, a majority of the interviewees expressed how their children were different from other Somali children because they are academically strong and have good manners. They wanted their children to be treated differently, mainly because they feel they are very involved parents, and their children are not newcomers or ELLs. Idil said, "They treat her like ESL. She is born here, and she is smart girl. It takes them little time to realize that. I also tell the teachers at the beginning of the year about my kids."

Similar to many other parents, participants separate their own children from "those other children" who are not as well-mannered or smart as their children within the Somali community.

The School's Expectations

In Portland Schools, parents who do not speak English must make appointments with interpreters and teachers in order to talk to the teachers. Unlike the majority of Somali parents, all interviewees communicate with the schools and the teachers of their children in English. The ability to speak English allows parents to visit the schools without the need to wait for an interpreter. However, that is not the case for most Somali parents. Even those who can communicate in English value the presence of an interpreter. Rahma, who communicates with teachers in English, said, "Sometimes they find me an interpreter, especially when someone is available. Other times, they encourage me to use my English. The alternative is to make an appointment." Lack of language facilitation at the schools influences language minorities' parental involvement.

Interviewees suspect that schools intentionally do not want them to attend school events in order to avoid committing resources to provide interpreters for parents. They believe that they are excluded because of their status as

159

language minority and/or due to their socioeconomic status. Rahma speculates by saying, "I am not sure if the schools want people who do not speak English to come to school meetings. It will require from them to bring interpreters. Maybe they do not want us to be part of the parent organizations." Dowlo believes the issue has something to do with socioeconomics. She said, "No one wants to help the poor." This perception of exclusion influences Somali parents' parental involvement negatively.

Teachers' Expectations

When it comes to teachers' expectations, only 50% of the Somali parents who took the survey reported that they strongly agree that their children's teachers want them to participate in the schooling of their children. The percentage went up to 90% of the survey respondents when they were asked about the expectation of the religious teacher. Also, three out of the five interviewees believe that the teachers want them to participate in the schooling process of their children. Farah uses teachers' statements to support his perception. He said, "When I see them, they give me their contact information. They say 'email me' or 'call me.' I consider that as an invitation to communicate." At the same time, the parent participants reported that they do not understand what the teachers expect from them. He said, "I

160

do not know the ways they want me to be involved." However, one of the five participants noted that at the elementary level, teachers invite parents to the classroom more than middle school teachers. She believes that teachers asked parents to be involved at the lower grades because the events were low key. Dowlo said, "They invited us to pumpkin festivals." Rahma, who considered herself very involved, questioned how parents volunteering in the school cafeteria correlates to educational outcomes. In short, while more than half of the participants believe that the teachers at the school want them to participate, they show a lack of understanding of the process and question how their volunteering at the school is helping or could help their children.

Children's Attitudes to their Parents' School Involvement

All interviewees reported that their children are doing well academically. They emphasized that their children's academic performance is positively correlated to their parental involvement. However, their understanding of parental involvement is limited to coming to the schools of their children only when they are invited and helping their children with the homework or getting academic assistance for them.

Additionally, results of the survey and interviews indicate that parents believe their middle school children do not want them to be involved in their schools. Participants believe that their middle school children are at a developmental stage that makes them resist their parents' school involvement. Idil said, "And my daughter, understandably does not want me to be at the school." However, more parents reported that their children want them to participate in their religious education. Parents' perceptions about their children's attitude toward their involvement in their middle schools influence negatively their intentions and behaviors regarding their parental involvement.

As mentioned above, Somali parents' intentions and behaviors regarding their involvement in the schools of their children are influenced by their perception of the views of relevant groups. These groups include Somali community members, educators, and their own children. The data show that parents believe that members of their community expect them to be involved in their children's education and schools while the schools as institutions and their own children do not want them to be involved in the schools for different reasons. Both survey respondents and interviewees were divided on the issue of teachers' expectations.

In the next section, I will use the third construct of TPB, perceived behavioral controls, and how these perceived controls influence Somali parents' intentions and behaviors regarding their parental involvement in their children's education and schools.

Perceived Behavioral Controls

According to TPB, perceived behavioral controls are defined as aspects of a person's life that they see as contributing to the ease or difficulty of engaging in a particular behavior. For the purpose of this study, perceived behavioral controls are what Somali parents who participated in this study perceive as having an effect on their participation in their children's education and schooling. The data show lack of knowledge of the system, inability to speak English, lack of time to go to the schools, child care commitments, types of employment, feelings of being outsiders, and lack of communication between the schools and parents are the main perceived controls which influence negatively Somali parents' involvement in their children's schools.

Seventy percent of Somali parents who took the survey reported the existence of barriers to their parental involvement, while only 60% of respondents reported the existence of opportunities for their parental involvement. In

163

the interview, I asked the participants the types of barriers and opportunities that they believe influenced their parental involvement. Lack of understanding of the U.S. education system, safety concerns, language, childcare, time, and lack of communication were the major barriers. Ability to understand English and teachers' attitudes were the opportunities for some of the Somali parents who participated in the study.

All interviewees said that they do not understand the U.S. education system. Dowlo said "I do not know how to participate." They want to learn about the system and navigate it in order to serve their children. Jama believes "The person [parent] should know the 'how.' How the system works. Then that time, he can help the children." Ironically, with this perceived limited understanding, the results of both the quantitative and the qualitative data show that Somali parents consider themselves involved in their children's education. Their involvement encompasses academic and non-academic activities. They reported that they attend parent-teacher conferences and find assistance for their children. They also take their children to the libraries.

Parents also reported that their children do not access the community centers and public libraries to get help with their school homework due to safety concerns. Farah said, "I do not want to send my children to the community centers. There are drug dealers and bad people in the neighborhood." Parents' concerns about safety and their reluctance to send their children to the community centers influences their involvement. This concern prevents the children from getting free academic assistance and means parents have to seek alternative ways to find academic assistance for their children. They argue that schools should provide safe after-school environments so that the children can do their homework. Farah said, "I hope they will have after-school programs for the kids." In fact, some Somali parents do not let their children take the school bus due to safety concerns. They want to keep their children away from the bad influences of some of their peers. Idil said, "The bad kids always influence the good ones. In America they will keep everyone in the same place. That is why I do not send my kids with the bus."

The ability of the research participants to communicate in English and their relatively high educational attainment were not good predictors of their involvement in their children's schools. They perceive that their English is far from perfect, so that they are unable to express their ideas as a native English speaker. Jama said, "I have communication issue sometimes. I do not speak English as a native. I have moments when I do not understand the conversations." Inability to speak English or lacking the confidence to use English limits the parental involvement in schools of language minorities.

Additionally, participants reported that having to take care of younger children was a barrier to their participation in their children's education. However, despite these challenges, all participants reported that they manage to attend parent-teacher conferences and go to school anytime they are invited. Idil said, "I have to ask/beg my neighbors to watch my kids while I attend conferences."

All parents who were interviewed believe that there is disconnection between school and parents. Parents reported that the schools communicate with parents when the children are in the elementary grades. At the middle school level, the only call they get is when their children get in trouble. Idil said, "In the past they call us to come and join them for field trips and school events. Now, no communication." They voice the need for more communication between parents and schools. Jama made a suggestion: "They must consider us as partners. I mean like what they do with the white people."

As mentioned before, Somali parents' beliefs about education and their interactions with school systems are mainly shaped by their beliefs, behavioral/subjective norms, and control beliefs. The constructs of TPB (beliefs, subjective norms, and behavioral control) lead to intentions, or lack of them, and subsequent behaviors. In the following section, I will share the intentions and behaviors of Somali parents toward the schools or their children.

Somali Parents Intentions and Behavior Towards Parental Involvement

The first constructs of the TPB (behavioral beliefs, normative beliefs, and control beliefs) lead to or prevent intentions and behaviors. According TPB an intention is an indication of an individual's readiness to perform a given behavior, while a behavior is an individual's observable responses. In this study, intentions and the behaviors refer to Somali parents' parental involvement in their middle school children's schools. Parental involvement is defined as parental work with children in education and in schools and with educators to make sure their children succeed. I placed intentions and behaviors in one section because all survey respondents and interviewees said that they have intentions to be involved in their children's education and schooling. However, the question become whether their intentions resulted in actual behaviors.

Somali parents who participated in the study showed an interest in their children's education and schools. All parents who responded to the survey have intentions to participate more in their children's education and schools. However, according to the survey results, Somali parents who took the survey are far more involved in their children's education in general and less involved in their children's schools. For example, all twenty parents who took the survey talk to their children about education, meet their religious school teachers, and help their children with Koran homework, while only three out of twenty parents reported they volunteered at their children's schools, and only one person out of twenty attends fieldtrips. According to the survey results, involvement of the Somali parents who participated in the study in their children's schools was limited to attending parent teacher conferences, yet all twenty parents said they are very involved in their children's schools. In other words, they are actually less involved in the schools of their children than they think. Or they have different definitions and perceptions of parental participation in the schools of their children.

Similar conclusions can be drawn from the interview results. According to the five interviewees, all of them are involved in their children's education and schools. However, the actual behaviors of each participant were different. This difference in actual behaviors highlights the diversity within

168

the sample and is a manifestation of how dealing with the general population (Somali parents of middle school children in Portland, Maine) as monolithic is ineffective.

Dowlo and Rahma who are the least educated of the interviewees are most involved, while Idil and the two male university graduates, Jama and Farah were least involved in their children's schools. However, all five participants reported that they are more involved in their children's Koran schools, help their children with their homework, attend parent teacher conferences, and get academic assistance for their children.

All parents who were interviewed said that they are every involved in their children's Koranic schools. They said they volunteer at the Koranic school, and communicate with the teachers frequently. Rahmo and Dowlo said they believe the reason they are so involved in the Koranic schools is because the Koranic teachers understand them. "We are on the same page. It is always different than the way I deal with public school teachers. I trust the *Dugsi*/Koran teachers more. We speak the same language" (Dowlo).

All Somali parents interviewed believe they should and intend to help their children with their homework. But many find they cannot complete the behavior as the content becomes more difficult and complex. Most of the parents reported that they used to help their children with the homework when they were young, but now they cannot help them because of the complexity of the content. Farah said, "I am not good at middle school math." However, he mentioned that he has structures in place so that the older children help the younger ones with the homework. So his intention is fulfilled in another way. Rahma and Idil get academic assistance in the form of tutoring for their children, and Jama not only encourages his children to seek help from the teachers but also helps them to find the help they need. He says, "I do not know the content or the subject. I find for them someone who can help them most of the time." It is clear that Somali parents who were interviewed use different means to get academic assistance for their children. "Sometimes I cannot help them," said Jama.

Only Rahma and Dowlo who are the least educated of all participants reported that they monitor their children's grades online. Ironically, they expressed that they understand the grading system. Dowlo said, "I look at their grades. I understand the different standards like 2, 3, and 4. I know which one is a better grade." She mentioned that she created an email account so that the teachers can email her about her child's grades and performances. Both women articulated that monitoring of their children's grades is an effective parental

170

involvement strategy. Rahma said, "I went to the school after I saw my son's grade." In addition, she said, "My son was getting after-school help 3 days every week until he made up all his work."

Dowlo and Rahma not only attend parent teacher conferences, monitor and understand grades, and request to meet teachers but they also advocate for their children. Both women schedule meetings with their children's teachers whenever they realize that their children are not doing well academically. Sometimes they show up at the school and request to meet the teachers. They are reluctant to wait for interpreters and use their English to expedite the meetings. The women said that they protect and advocate for their children. Rahma reported how one school administrator misrepresented facts to implicate her son. "The assistant principal even mischaracterizes my son to implicate him. The social worker is much better than the assistant principal". Similarly, Dowlo reports how teachers want to put the children in trouble. "Teachers ask kids to apologize. Say sorry. They ask the kids to write their apology on paper. They want to put it in his record. Teachers and schools are against the poor people." At some point, Rahma reported that she volunteered at her son's cafeteria as another way to monitor his schooling experience.

Compared to Dowlo and Rahma, Idil, Jama, and Farah were less involved in their children's schools. Idil said she attends parent teacher conferences and the Open House to alert teachers about her daughter's aptitude and explains how she is smarter than English language learners. "I tell the teachers that she is not an ELL student." Jama, is very involved in his children's education. Besides attending parent teacher conferences, he advises his son to talk to his teachers and seek their help when he does not understand the material. Farah expects his wife to do most of the education and school involvement. He said he provides for his children all the materials they need and advises them. He does not have time to help his children with their homework and believes that the community centers in his neighborhood are unsafe. He asks his older children to help the younger ones with the homework.

In the next section, I present the findings of the investigation. In the process, I will look at the patterns of involvement from the standpoint of Theory of Planned behavior (TPB). The theory will help explain how beliefs, normative beliefs, and perceived controls influence these intentions and actual behaviors.

Findings of the Study

Finding #1: Somali Parents who Participated in the Study Demonstrated Different Levels and Types of Parental Involvement

Participants said they only go to schools when the teachers invite them. They said that both teachers and their own children do not like them to come to the school unexpectedly. Additionally, they do not want to disturb the learning and the teaching processes. However, when you look at participants' actual behavior, they are divided. Idil, Jama, and Farah are true to the separation of parent and teacher roles and do not visit the schools except when they are invited to attend the parent teacher conferences, while Dowlo and Rahma show up at the schools without appointments and meet with teachers. Rahma went further by volunteering at her son's school cafeteria. This is an indication that beliefs do not necessarily lead to or prevent individuals performing certain behaviors. Dowlo and Rahmo said they believe teachers are in charge of all school matters, yet this belief does not prevent them from getting involved in the schools of their children.

Finding #2: Somali Parents who Participated in this Study Share Common and Strong Beliefs Regarding Education, Schooling, and Parental Involvement

According to TPB, beliefs are defined as: individual's belief about consequences of particular behavior. All Somali parents who participated in the study expressed their beliefs and perceptions about education and schooling. Both survey respondents and interviewees view education and schooling as very important in their children's lives. They believe their children can do well only by acquiring knowledge from public and religious schools. Farah said, "People in the entire world seek education for better tomorrow." They also view their involvement in their children's education and schooling as essential.

According to the Somali parents who participated in the study, teachers are respected and will make important decision; parents are secondary to teachers. To them, teachers are responsible for teaching discipline and advising students. Rahma said, "Teachers were like parents and took care of all school related issues." They reported that parents' role was to prepare their children for the school by providing for them the materials they need for school. Dowlo said, "My mother was involved in my education. She used to buy for me all my need for the school." Rahma expressed her parents'

174

involvement in her education and schools. She said, "My parents were involved in my education. Without their participation I could not learn anything. You need uniforms, books, and everything."

Somali parents who participated in the study perceive themselves as involved parents, and 100% of the survey respondents and interviewees said parental involvement in schools and in education in general are very important. It is clear that Somali parents who participated in the study have perceptions about parental involvement. This perception is different from what participation in schools means in the U.S. In other words; the participants are more involved in their children's education and not in the schools. However, the most common beliefs among the participants are: only teachers are responsible for school matters; parents visit schools only when invited by teachers; and teachers and students do not like parents to come to the schools.

The participants of the study perceive that their community norms encourage education and their involvement in their children's education. Normative beliefs are defined as: the combination of perceived expectations from relevant individuals and groups and the intentions to comply with these expectations. Normative beliefs influence Somali parents' intentions and behaviors regarding their parental involvement in their children's schools. Eighty percent of the parents who took the survey indicated that Somali community members expect them to participate in their children's schools. All interviewees also expressed the same belief. The sense of group feeling is evident in their use of the terms "we" and "us" to describe the Somali community in Portland, Maine. "We do not know how to be involved" (Dowlo). "They do not want us to be involved" (Dowlo). "We are a poor community" (Jama). Perhaps this group feeling explains why Somalis in the U.S and other western countries cluster in the same areas. Articulating the community expectations and the desire to meet these expectations influence Somali parents' involvement in their children's education and schools. However, if we look at the actual behavior of the Somali parents who participated in the study, the majority of their involvement is in education and outside of the schools. Yet, all participants said that Somali community members consider them very involved in both their children's schools and education. This brings up the question: How do Somali community/parents define parental involvement in schools?

Finding #3: There are some Beliefs, Perceptions, and Norms that Appear to Create Doubt or Discourage School Involvement of Somali Parents

According to TPB, some normative beliefs may lead to intentions and behavior. However, the results of the investigation show other normative beliefs influence negatively parents' intentions and behaviors regarding parental involvement in their children's schools. The participants indicated that both the teachers and their own middle school children do not want them to be involved in their public schools. Dowlo who is most involved participants said, "They call us only for pumpkin festival. These is the things they want me involved. Not the important ones. They do not call me for the important meetings. They do not want my ideas." Jama and Farah said that they do not go to the schools of their children because they do not want to interrupt the teaching. They said that the teachers will contact us when they need us. This is an indication that Somali parents are not involved because they perceive that the teachers do not want them. Whether it is the reality or mere perception, the consequence of this perception damages the educative process of the students. According to the data, expectations of religious schoolteachers also influence positively the participation of Somali parents in their children's religious schools.

Finding #4: **Some** Perceived Behavioral Controls Discourage Parental Involvement

Perceived behavioral control beliefs are Somali parents' beliefs about the ease or difficulty of participating in their children's schools. Survey respondents and participants indicated the existence of some obstacles to their public school participation. These difficulties influence their parental involvement in their children's schools. Inability to speak English, lack of time, poor communication between the parents and the schools, child care commitment, and general feeling of being an outside are the common difficulties that negatively influence Somali parents' intentions regarding their participation in their children's schools. However, ability to understand and speak English was also seen as a positive influence/perceived opportunity to their intentions and behavior. Rahma, for example goes to her son's school and is able to communicate with teachers in English when the school cannot find an interpreter for her. Idil, Jama, and Farah are more educated and speak English better than the other two participants. They could communicate with teachers in English. Yet, they do not pursue this opportunity. Maybe (unlike Dowlo and Raham) their children do not get

178

in trouble at their schools and that makes them stay away
from the schools unless they are invited.

Finding #5: TPB Does Not Explain the Entire Dynamic Process of Beliefs, Norms, and Perceived Controls Leading to Intentions and then to Behaviors

I used the Theory of Planned Behavior to explain how
beliefs, norms, and perceived controls of Somali parents who
participated in this study demonstrated the intentions and
behaviors to be become involved (or not involved) in their
children's education and schools. The theory was very
helpful to explain the links between beliefs and intentions
and actual behavior. The progression from beliefs to
intentions to actual behaviors was not complete in some
cases. In other words, in the case of the study participants, the
interactions of the factors were more dynamic than linear.
The theory only goes so far in explaining what is happening
for these Somali families. Some participants said they
believe in one thing and did the opposite, while others were
true to their beliefs. Similarly, some parents reported that the
teachers and their children did not want them to be involved
in the schools. However, two of the parents did not comply
with these expectations from these relevant groups. They are
pro-active on behalf of their children; they go to the schools
and demand to meet the teachers. Additionally, all

179

participants expressed their ability to speak English as an opportunity, and the lack of time, other commitments such as their jobs or the lack of childcare as barriers to their involvement in their children's schools.

Having provided this analysis of the data using the Theory of Planned Behavior and the major findings of the investigation, in the following chapter, I summarize the study and its limitations, discuss the findings in light of the literature on parental involvement in schools and present the implications of the study for theory and practice. In addition, I make some recommendations for further study of this topic.

CHAPTER SIX
DISCUSSION OF THE FINDINGS AND
IMPLICATIONS

In this chapter, I begin with an overview of the study and the methodology I employed. The limitations of the study and a discussion of the findings in relation to current literature and research with regard to parental involvement and engagement of language minority parents follow these sections. I then discuss the implications of the study for practitioners and research communities. I end the chapter with my concluding thoughts.

Overview of the Study

The problem this study addresses is rooted in the context of the large Somali community in Portland, Maine and the challenges presented by such demographic changes in the city's school system. This overview attempts to highlight the significance of my research and its far-reaching implication for both policy and practice.

Close to ten thousand Somalis came to Southern Maine from 1994 to 2014. This influx of Somali refugees in Portland and Lewiston, Maine has significantly changed the demographic landscape of the southern part of the state. As a result of these changes, the composition of the student

181

population in the two cities has changed. Somali students make up around 10% of the student population in Portland. The Portland school district is faced with legal demands and challenges in dealing with the new students and their families. Preparing educators to meet the educational needs of the students remains one of the most immediate challenges. Other challenges for schools and communities are economic, political, and social.

Part of preparing educators to meet the educational needs of the students is to establish a knowledge base about this new group of students and their families. Current practice for meeting language minority students' educational needs is based on the commonly held belief that parental involvement in schools is important to the learning of children (Christenson & Sheridan, 2001). In addition, educational systems in the U.S have traditionally treated language minority students and their families as essentially the same and, in fact, have developed policies based on research and models from schools with large Spanish speaking students and their families. The notion of treating all language minority students and their families similarly despite within and across group diversity is ineffective at least and counterproductive at times (Barrera, 2006; Hosp & Reshchly, 2004). So the study adds to the existing body of knowledge about parental involvement of language minority students by focusing on Somali parents' views of education and schooling and their involvement in their children's schools

Purpose of the Study

The purpose of this mixed method investigation was to explore perceptions of parents of Somali children who are in Portland Public Schools regarding education and schooling of their children and the intentions and behavior of these parents regarding their involvement in their children's education and schooling. For the purpose of this study, *parental involvement* was defined as parental work with children in education and in schools and with educators to make sure their children succeed. The term *education* was defined as the act of preparing children intellectually for a productive life. It encompasses many aspects of the educative process of children including public and religious schooling, while *schooling* is defined as institutionalization of education in grades and with a curriculum. The above definitions were essential to clarify my definition of the terms to the participants and to the reader.

The study builds on Crespo-Jimenez's (2010) study, which examined the patterns of involvement of Latino parents with middle school children in the education process. The exploration was accomplished through surveys and personal interviews with Somali parents. The study was guided by the following research questions:

RQ 1. How do first generation Somali parents of middle school students who are part of a refugee population settled in Portland, Maine view education and schooling?

RQ 2. How are first generation Somali parents who are part of a refugee population settled in Portland, Maine involved in their middle school children's education in general and schooling in particular and what factors influence their involvement?

In my initial design, there was a third research question: RQ 3. What are the perceptions of Somali parents of middle school students who are part of a refugee population settled in Portland, Maine whose children are or have been part of English Language Learners (ELL) programs with regard to the expectations of their children and the responsibilities of parents in the school? However, after the participant recruitment process, I realized that the sample selected for the interviews did not meet the conditions in this research question. The participants for this study have children who have exited or were never a part of English Language Learners programs. So, the investigation did not address the third research question although it did provide

184

findings on Somali parents' perceptions of view and the schools' view of the responsibilities of parents.

Methodology

The research questions required a general understanding of the perceptions of Somali parents who participated in the study. This general understanding was achieved by studying individual cases and interpreting experiences from the participants' expressed perceptions (Stake, 1995). To explore the above-mentioned research questions, I followed a mixed method design to describe the perceptions of Somali parents of middle school children about education, schooling, and parental involvement. The methods included surveys and interviews of twenty Somali parents of middle school children. I employed a framework rooted in psychological research: The Theory of Planned Behavior (TPB).

Icek Ajzen's Theory of Planned Behavior involves three components which lead to intentions and behaviors: Attitudes/beliefs about the behavior, normative beliefs, and perceived behavioral control (Ajzen, 1991). Beliefs about the behavior stem from whether the person has negative or positive evaluations toward performing a specific behavior. Normative beliefs refer to what the person believes other people and groups who are important to him or her will think

185

about whether or not the person should perform the behavior and what these individuals and groups are doing regarding the same behavior. Perceived behavioral control is a person's perceived ease or difficulty in performing a behavior because of other intervening factors. Together these three components shape an individual's behavioral intentions and behaviors.

The data for the case studies came from surveys and interviews. The sampling technique was purposeful. Potential participants were approached in their homes and community centers. The population of this study was limited to Somali parents of middle school children in Portland Public Schools. In the first phase of the data collection, twenty parents of middle school children (13 women and 7 men) were selected to take a survey. The surveys and the interview protocol were available to all subjects in Somali and English. Similarly, consent letters and the study overview were available in both languages, Somali and English. In the second phase, five of the original twenty parents who took the survey were interviewed. A series of three interviews was conducted with each parent. The interview protocol and the survey were designed to elicit insights into aspects of the research questions and the constructs of TPB.

The data obtained from the surveys informed and created the context for the interviews. I followed quantitative

186

traditional methods to interpret the survey data. I presented the survey results in tables and graphs as well as in descriptive form. During the study processes I maintained comprehensive and detailed record keeping. I employed techniques such as journaling and translating data to English in order to capture participants' views accurately. I conducted member checking of my interpretations in the third interview. I analyzed the survey and presented data in tables and charts. For the qualitative section, I coded data manually by using constructs of the framework as labels and developed categories by using the study's conceptual framework. The unit of analysis or the objects that were analyzed were Somali parents of middle school children. However, the main objective was to analyze the responses of each case (parent) and identify the commonalities and the diversity among the cases to create a narrative. I used the emerging categories to describe the perception of Somali parents of middle school children about education and schools and their views of parental involvement with regard to those. I shared the categories and the themes with the study participants to enhance the validity and accuracy.

All interviews were audio-recorded and my initial reactions to the interview were documented within 48 hours. Transcripts of each interview were quickly translated from

187

Somali to English, transcribed, and analyzed to answer the research questions and to explore further questions and themes for the next interview. Interviews were spaced to allow time for the previous data to be translated, transcribed, and analyzed in preparation for the next phase.

In summary, the data analysis stemmed from information provided by the participants in responding to questions in the survey and during semi-structured interviews. The data obtained from the survey were analyzed using quantitative methods, while the data obtained from the interviews were presented first in a narrative format. A thematic analysis of the narrative section provided details and insights about the perceptions these participants have about their own schooling, their involvement in their children's schools, and experience with institutions of learning in the U.S. The thematic analysis was useful in connecting the individual narratives to the collective story of the participants through the research questions and the conceptual framework of the study.

Limitations

There are several limitations to this study. Some of these research limitations are also strengths including the community insider status of the researcher. These limitations also include methodological, theoretical, and practical aspects of the study. First, as a native of Somalia and an educator in the Portland Schools, I have strong relationships with the Somali community. My status as an insider and community leader and my affiliation with the school system could have influenced the participants' responses. I tried hard to explain my role as a researcher during the data collection. However, it was not easy for some interviewees who have known me for more than ten years to consider me in the role of researcher. They often addressed me as one of their own (a Somali) and at times as their advocate and representative in the school system. As an advantage, my relationship with the participants may have encouraged the interviewees and survey respondents to participate in the study and share their ideas because they consider me as one of their own. Furthermore, my identity and connection allowed me to understand and capture nuances in language and feelings. These advantages may have added value and efficiency to the research process.

Second, my limited experience with research and as a speaker of English as a second language could be limiting factors. Of course, the potential of committing errors is very high in the case of novice student researchers. Translating interviews and field notes accurately from Somali to English was a challenging task with potential errors. I did conduct

189

member checks in the third interview to help ensure accuracy of my interpretation. In addition to my status as a student researcher and my previous training as an experimental physical scientist and non-native speaker of English, the complexity of the topic requires more research than my graduate thesis can attempt.

Third, interviewing as a method of research has its advantages and disadvantages. Allowing subjects to reconstruct their experiences and express their views can be achieved through interviews (Seidman, 2006). Yet, I recognize my potential bias in all stages of the research, including the fieldwork stage. Although extra care was required at the analysis and interpretation stage, I examined my role as researcher throughout the entire process by allowing the data to emerge from the participants, working intentionally to limit my familiarity with the circumstances, and bracketing my inner latent feelings as a native of Somalia and as a teacher in the Portland Public Schools so as not to personally influence the research process. Also, the nature of the data collected through interviews is highly subjective, thus, open to interpretation and uncertainties about meaning. Yet my analytic training has helped me to systematically analyze for themes and to hold my biases in check

In addition, the Theory of Planned Behavior could be viewed as a limitation of this study. The model is very good in identifying factors that contribute to explicit behaviors. However, it is limited in identifying emotions in relation to intentions and behavior. For example, the study shows that Somali parents feel that they do not have an effect on their children's schools, and TPB does not measure the sense of efficacy.

Finally, the study is limited by the small sample size of five Somali parents of middle school children who volunteered to participate in the study. The data are limited to a single, brief survey and to three interviews with each of five parents. Nevertheless, I tried to ensure the interviews were rich in information. I used Somali language to ask the questions, asked probing questions, and conducted member checking. I also tried hard to ensure diversity in the sample to achieve representation of Somali parents of middle school children in Portland, Maine. The number of women was more than the number of men, because women make up the majority of Somali parents in Portland, Maine. However, the information gathered in this investigation cannot be generalized to represent all Somali parents because of the sample size.

Nevertheless, the study does provide information about these new immigrants to the U.S. about which little has been written. And the study employed all the expected protections for the participants, furthermore, the data were carefully collected and analyzed to provide a trustworthy picture of this sample of the population.

Discussion of the Findings

In this section, the findings of the study are discussed in relation to the existing literature regarding parental involvement in schools of language minorities. The original conceptual framework of the study is used as a guide for the discussion. The weaving of the findings obtained from the surveys and the interviews with the current research on the topics of parental involvement of language minority parents in general and Somali parents in particular contributes to an understanding of the complexities of interacting with language minority parents and educating their children effectively.

Perceptions of Parental Involvement

When it comes to parental engagement in schooling, immigrant parents have different demographic profiles from parents who often are disengaged from their children's schooling. (Davis-Kean, 2005; Pena, 2000). In this study, Somali parents reported that they are involved in their children's school. However, their involvement was limited to parenting, supplying the students' needs for school, and helping students with their homework. They also attend parent teacher conferences and whenever the teachers invite them to the schools. Somali parents are not involved in decision-making and, generally, do not volunteer in their children's schools. Although their limited/different involvement can be due to various factors, there is a need to revisit the term "parental involvement" in schools by exploring what it means to educators and schools as well as to parents of different backgrounds.

Somali parents' beliefs about their roles and the role of the teachers, their children's attitude towards their involvement, unfamiliarity with the complex systems of schools, and other barriers, such as lack of time and unwelcome school culture, all influence Somali parents' ability and willingness to be involved in the schools of their children. In spite of these barriers, some Somali parents were able to participate more formally than the others. Dowlo and Rahma visit their children's schools to meet teachers and monitor grades online. In fact, Rahma reported that she volunteered to help the cafeteria staff during the lunch in her child's school. It appeared that for both of these women the need to be present in the school for their children overcame their reluctance to be involved in this way.

Somali parents who participated in this study said they respect teachers. According to their traditions, teachers are well respected (Farid & McMahan, 2004). They reported that schooling is separate from parenting, and their role as parents is to prepare students for school. This explains the resistance of parents in the study to be proactive in their children's schooling. Instead of becoming fully involved in their children's schools as educators in the U.S. system expect, these parents reported that they engage their children in home learning and express their expectation to their children. According to them, teachers are responsible for what takes place in the schools, and they come to schools when they are invited. Nevertheless, Rahma and Dowlo were more involved than others. This required an unusual amount of courage and drive to see their children succeed.

In previous research, parents' level of education was found to be a limiting factor to parental involvement (Floyd, 1998; Sosa, 1997). Ironically, in the case of this study's participants, parents' level of education was not a limiting factor to parental involvement in the schools of their children. Rather, the least educated parents were the most involved in their children's education. The reason for the enhanced

194

involvement of the less educated participants in the schools of their children might be they did not have enough previous successful experience with schools in their country. In other words, they did not need to unlearn old habits/experiences. Another reason could be that their children's experiences with schools may make them feel as if they should be involved to ensure good behavior of their kids. Both Rahma and Dowlo reported that their sons got in trouble in their schools.

The diversity within the study participants regarding their involvement in schools and their perceptions that they are 100% involved raise questions about the actual definition and measurement of parental involvement. This discrepancy was highlighted in the past (Fan & Chen, 2001). They questioned the definition and the method of measuring parental involvement in schools (Fan & Chen, 2001).

Community expectation influences individual's behavior (Azjen, 1985). Somali parents who participated in the study reported that their community members expect them to become involved in their children's schools. As a Somali, I see Somalis as a cohesive community. They move to the same cities and neighborhoods and influence each other's behavior. According to the findings of this investigation, Somali parents' perceptions about their

195

community's expectations regarding school involvement can be helpful in designing appropriate strategies for engaging parents. However, it is not clear whether the community expectation applies to being involved in education more than in schooling. Additionally, Somali community does not have organizations for helping parents understand how to navigate through the US schooling process.

Student's age and grade level are found to influence parental involvement in schools. Generally, parents are more involved at the elementary level (Floyd, 1998). Somalis have high expectations for their children. In Somalia, children are considered to be adults at the age of 15. In Somali tradition, being an adult means the individual is responsible to not only manage his affairs but also to take care of his parents and younger siblings. Many Somali people in the U.S. exercise this tradition.

Additionally, Somali parents who participated in the study reported that their children do not want them to be involved. In other words, perceptions about child development and children's attitude toward their parents' involvement in their schools are limiting factors to parental involvement of Somali parents. Educators need to realize that teenage minority children (like white teen age children) do not want their parents to be involved in their schools. In

196

addition, educators need to understand the perceptions of Somali parents regarding child development and expectations.

Lack of time and other commitments, such as childcare and inability to speak English, were also expressed as limiting factors to parental involvement. This is not unique to Somali parents. Mexicans, Dominican, and Puerto Rican families expressed similar concerns (Crespo-Jimenez, 2010; Scribner, 1999). Teachers and school leaders must recognize these circumstances and consider working with parents to overcome barriers in order to encourage greater involvement in the schools.

Perhaps, the most common barrier to parental involvement is lack of familiarity with the system. Parents are more involved when they know the expectation of the schools and the teachers. When there is lack of understanding between the school's expectations regarding parents and the parents' expectations of their roles, the school culture can be seen as insensitive and incompetent at accommodating the needs of a diverse community. Traditionally, parents who were schooled in the U.S understand the expectations better than the newcomers. Many newcomers, including Somalis, do not have a good understanding of the educational system, which many white middle-class families enjoy. Newcomers usually do not have the same background to understand the culturally unspoken rules. For example, some Latino groups define parental involvement in school as helping students with their homework (Arias & Morillo-Cambell, 2008), while American teachers expect parents to attend school-sponsored events (Crespo-Jimenes, 2010). Similarly, in this study, Somalis limit parental involvement in schools to buying school needs for students, helping them with their homework, and attending parent-teacher conferences.

Differing Views of the Roles of Teachers and Parents in Students' Schooling

Studies have been conducted to explain why so many students from one language minority group (Spanish speaking) are failing in schools. Some studies suggest correlations between poor achievement of minority students and lack of involvement of language minority parents in their children's school without asking questions about the causes of their limited involvement (Scribner, 1999; Zentella, 2002). However, studies show that language minority subgroups value education and believe that they are involved even though the majority of minority students in general (including language minority) perform below grade level in standardized exams (Orfield, Losen, Wald, & Swanson, 2004).

Somali parents, like Mexican, Dominican, and Puerto Rican families, care about the education of their children and believe that they are very involved (Crespo-Jimenez, 2010). Somali parents who participated in this study said they value education and send their children to school for a better future. Sending children to schools and preparing them to become productive in their adult life is a generally accepted purpose of education (Ogbu, 1978). Somali parents do not believe that they have a role within school affairs. They believe that only teachers and students are responsible for teaching and learning in the school. Some of the participants in this study realize that they must step out of their role as Somali parent and meet the expectations of the schools even though they do not see it as best practice in their culture.

The fact that the parents in this study conflated the terms "education" and "schooling" shows that there are many misunderstandings at the base of the unrealized expectations of educators and the sense on the part of parents that they are very involved. Providing materials, transportation, extra-mural experiences, and encouragement are very much a part of supporting children's education. Even the research on this topic does not fully appreciate this aspect of parental involvement. It is another reason to rethink the definition of parental involvement in schools and education, and the roles of parents and educators.

Research shows parental involvement in schools is an effective intervention to mitigate low student performance. According to Epstein (2001) and Christensen and Sheridan, (2001), students do better in schools when parents and teachers collaborate on children's education. This collaboration between parents and schools can only be achieved when there are common understandings of the expectations from all sides. Learning from and about each other and acknowledging and mitigating differences are essential ingredients for better collaboration. Epstein (2001) argues educators and families must work together for better student outcomes. She defines parental involvement as a collaborative relationship in which parents and teachers are engaged in sharing not only information but also expertise and influence.

According to Epstein (2001), schools must educate parents in parenting, establish from-and-to school communication, recruit parents to volunteer at school and to teach the children at home, involve them in decision-making, and help families navigate community resources. However, Dr. Epstein's "overlapping spheres approach" defines parental involvement in schools in Western middle-class terms and risks the creation of a deficit model regarding parental involvement of some language minority groups who define parental involvement differently. Such a model has a one-way orientation about how parents can be molded to fit into the existing pre-established patterns of parental involvement without engaging parents in the discussions. This orientation promotes teacher-centered practices and does not accept parents' version of parental involvements and teacher roles.

A reciprocal model to Epstein's typology can come out when teachers make no assumptions about families before knowing them. Additionally, teachers and families must be pulled together as a group to talk about the responsibilities and expectation of teachers and parents. One-to-one interaction with parents is a very important intervention and an alternative to a one-size-fits-all approach.

Expanding the Theory of Planned Behavior

The Theory of Planned Behavior (TPB) was useful in thinking about the relationship between social and cultural norms, beliefs, and personal desires; however, it doesn't help to explain all behaviors fully because of the emotional components that are not taken into consideration. For example, the study shows that Somali parents feel that they do not have an effect on their children's schools, and TPB

201

does not measure efficacy. As Farah said, "Who am I to tell them what they need to do?" They feel marginalized and targeted. For example, Dowlo reported the social workers and some teachers in her child's school want to implicate her son and other Somali children for negative behavior. Rahma thinks the assistant principal in her child's school targets her son.

In addition, the Theory of Planned Behavior addresses the psychological factors, which may influence intentions and actual behavior, but it does not account for specific knowledge of how to actually execute the behavior (Crespo-Jimenez, 2010). For example, participants of the study had intentions to be involved but do not know how to participate. "I want to be involved. I do not know how" (Rahma).

This study showed that barriers in fulfilling intentions to perform the behavior of parental involvement in schooling, or at least some aspects of it, often outweighed beliefs and norms. The results show that the pieces do not fall into place linearly. The dynamic that takes into consideration all of these factors is much more complex. Furthermore, there are other factors like emotions and lack of knowledge that had an effect on what the individuals in the study actually did. The results also showed that for each individual the psycho-social factors played out differently. In rethinking the conceptual framework of the study, I would add social issues such as class and authority that lead to feelings of lack of authority and lack of empowerment. Measuring or capturing Somali parents feelings regarding their children's schooling is essential in determining their intentions and behavior. The current conceptual frame work fails to address these important elements.

Implications

The results of the study can be helpful for establishing policies and practices to increase Somali parents' school involvement as well as provide avenues for further research.

Implications for Educators and School Leaders

Outreach to parents and brainstorming with them regarding ways they can collaborate with educators in their children's education is needed. Participants of this study made clear that they want to be involved; they need to be invited specifically and directly to the table. School administrators need to invite parents into the school. They have to ensure that their teachers practice cultural competence. Administrators need to make sure that teachers are encouraged to know and understand the ethnic diversity of their students, to meet parents in their homes, to continually work toward appreciating their students as individuals and learning as much as they can about them and their backgrounds.

Cultural competence is both a skill set and a disposition. It involves a shift in the way Western educators have been thinking about their roles vis a vis immigrant families. There must be a willingness to be curious about other people and their thinking and an openness to incorporating that understanding into their interactions and their teaching. Seeing that students and their families have "funds of knowledge" (Moll & Gonzalez, 2004; Scribner, 1999) that have been untapped as opposed to deficits in their knowledge and experience is critical to supporting the agency of parents to participate in the schooling, not just the education, of their children.

Additionally, school leaders need to design strategies to involve Somali parents in the schools. Inviting parents to the schools is not enough. They can invite parents to be part of parent advisory committees, make concerted efforts to seek out the opinions and attitudes of all parents, especially those whose voices are not often heard, and help parents, like the participants in this study, to be more engaged by helping them find concrete ways to engage in their child's schooling. School leaders must provide interpreters, engage parents in conversation about their perceptions and commitment regarding parental involvement, and put forward clear expectations for teachers and parents. Crespo-Jimenez (2010) suggests school leaders must help immigrant families learn about their new context and also allow them to bring their experiences to the table. Educational leaders need to embrace the full understanding of Epstein's spheres in encouraging minority and newcomer involvement. Perhaps, communication, collaboration, and decision-making are the most relevant elements when it comes to immigrant parents.

Americans believe that the public in public schools refers to who gets to go to school, but it is also about who makes decisions about schooling. Bringing families to the table means making them a part of the process of decision making (Epstein, 2001). They then can realize the point of view of others but also have their own views heard and respected. This gets at agency and thus understanding of how the American system works: it has rights and responsibilities, and they work best when there is full participation of all parties.

Also, the findings of this investigation help educators and researchers to examine stereotypical perceptions about language minority groups and their attitudes towards education. Teachers and educational leaders must avoid treating all minority groups homogeneously. Educators and school leaders need to understand the attitudes and expectations of Somali parents in order to avoid making inaccurate assumptions.

ELL and Special Education teachers can be good models for the kind of behavior all teachers should display. They emphasize family relationships and understand that there are various definitions of parental involvement. They appreciate the efforts taken to support the children on their caseloads. Like these teachers with their specific training and mindset, all educators need to show they care for their students and that they care and appreciate the adults who are doing what they do in the home. Educators have to meet people where they are…and also parents need to be encouraged to show what they know and what they do to support their children.

Implications for Educator and Educational Leader Preparation

Schools characterized by diverse students are the norm in many cities in the U.S. The idea of cultural competence is increasingly important for all educational practitioners. Thus teacher preparation programs as well as school leadership programs must take this issue seriously and provide more explicit coursework and experiences to bolster what in-service and pre-service students bring to the programs and to expand their understandings. This means depth of reading, of course, but also explorations of their beliefs and understandings and analysis of various experiences to ensure they are continually learning and adapting their practices appropriately. Action research done by practitioners or pre-service teachers is an effective way to learn more about communities and the various populations in it no matter what the population of any school is.

Maine is a rural, seemingly homogeneous state, but that is not an excuse for lack of attention to the diversity of ethnicity and socioeconomic status of students in a school. More explicit training in skills and enhancement of dispositions with regard to funds of knowledge of parents and communities are necessary. This study provides important lessons regarding the diversity we praise in America. In the twenty-first century, we need to move beyond assimilation and acculturation to appreciation of the differences we all represent. We want newcomers to be successful and that involves a certain amount of education about "how things are done here." But this kind of instruction and support of parents and children should not be at the expense of mutual sharing and trust in the cultures and views of those new to this country. We need to employ a "both/and" approach to welcoming our newest citizens or potential citizens and supporting them as they strive to learn in a very different institution of schooling.

To be "good villagers," Somali people want to make sure their own children and the children of their friends and relatives thrive. Teacher education programs must continually focus on what good teachers do to manage groups of children all the while seeing each child as an individual and each parent as a true partner in the entire enterprise of education and schooling. In other words, there is potential in approaching Somali parents as a unit because they view their community members as similar to them, an important notion for teacher educators as well as educational leaders to keep in mind.

Implications for Further Research

Overall, further research needs to done to examine how beliefs, norms, perceived behavioral controls, and emotions, feelings, and possibly other factors influence the intentions and behaviors of Somali parents regarding education, schools, and parental involvement. To take broad and inclusive views, multiculturalism and globalization are possible places to find theories or ideas that would help conceptualize what is going on here and aid in teasing out the complicated dynamic. Such ideas or theories may explain to all stakeholders the existence of different perspectives and how to promote cultural competence in our schools.

The sample size of this study was very small. Large and diverse samples may yield outcomes that would be more representative of the general population of Somalis in Portland, Maine. Additionally, the study took place in a relative small city compared to other cities like Minneapolis and Columbus with large Somali populations; studies in these locations would be a good addition to the literature on the subject.

This study was conducted with Somali parents. Crespo-Jimez (2010) study looked at Hispanic populations. It will be important to continue to investigate other immigrant populations as well, perhaps, as non-immigrant minority populations to provide a fuller picture to educators and scholars on the topic of parental involvement.

And, of course, this study presents a one-sided view, that of the parents. A larger study looking at educators' and school administrators' views and expectations as well as behaviors would enhance the scholarly research. I would recommend doing so for any any of several populations in a variety of locations.

The Epstein model, too, is definitely worth reexamining and conceptualizing in light of these results and my critique. I urge other scholars to develop and test other definitions and models of parental involvement so that a broader understanding of this important aspect of support for children might be more fully understood especially in light of the increasingly diverse school populations of this country.

REFERENCES

Abdikadir, F. &Cassanelli, L. (2007) "Somalia: Education in transition," *Bildhaan: An International Journal of Somali Studies*: Vol. 7, Article 7.

Ajzen, I. (1991). The theory of planned behavior. *Organizational behavior and human decision processes*, *50*(2), 179-211.

Ajzen, I., & Fishbein, M. (1980). Understanding attitudes and predicting social behavior. Englewood Cliffs, NJ: Prentice-Hall.

Arias, M. B., & Morillo-Campbell, M. (2008). Promoting ELL Parental Involvement: Challenges in Contested Times. *Online Submission*.

Arman, A. & Kapteijns, L. (2004) "Educating immigrant youth in the United States: An Exploration of the Somali case," *Bildhaan: An International Journal of Somali Studies*: Vol. 4, Article 6.

Artiles, A. & Klingner, J. K. (2007). Forging knowledge base on English language learners with special needs: Theoretical, population, and technical issues. *Teachers College Record, 108*(11), 2187-2194.

Argyris, C. (1959). *The individual and Organization: Some problems of mutual adjustment.* Administrative Science Quarterly, 2, 1-24.

Bacallao, M. L. (2005). *Entre dos mundos: How environmental systems influence acculturation and bicultural identity development in mexican adolescents.* (Order No. 3170396, The University of North Carolina at Chapel Hill). *ProQuest Dissertations and Theses,* 170-170 p. Retrieved from http://search.proquest.com.ursus-proxy1.ursus.maine.edu/docview/305424245?accountid=8120. (305424245).

Baker, A.J. & Soden, L.M. (1998, Sept.). The challenges of parent involvement research. New York: ERIC Clearinghouse on Urban Education. 9 pages. ED419030.

Ballantine, J. H., & Spade, J. Z. (2009). Social Science Theories on Teachers, Teaching, and Educational Systems. In *International Handbook of Research on Teachers and Teaching* (pp. 81-102). Springer US.

Banks C. & Banks J. (2003). *Multicultural education: Issues and perspectives*. (4thed). New York, NY: John Wiley and Sons.

Barrera, M. (2006).Roles of definitional and assessment model in the identification of new or second language learners of English for special education. *Journal of Learning Disabilities, 39*(2), 142-156.

Berry, J. W., Kim, U., & Boski, P. (1988). Psychological acculturation of immigrants' Cross-cultural adaptation: Current approaches (pp. 62-89). Thousand Oaks, CA: Sage Publications, Inc.

Brown v. Board of Educ., 347 U.S. 483 (1954)

213

Callahan, R. M. & Dabach, D. B. (2011). Rights versus reality: The Gap between civil rights and English learners' high school education opportunities. *Teachers College Record.* October, 2011.

Christensen, S.L., & Sheridan, S.M. (2001). *Schools and families.* New York, Guilford.

Crespo-Jimenez, M. (2010). Patterns of Latino Parental Involvement in Middle School: Case Studies of Mexican, Dominican and Puerto Rican Families.

Creswell, J. W. (2007). *Qualitative Inquiry research Design: Choosing Among Five Approaches* (Second Ed.). Thousand Oaks, California: Sage Publications.

Cutler, W. (2000). *Parents and schools.* Chicago: The University of Chicago Press, Ltd.

Davis-Kean, P. M (2005). The influence of parent's education and home income on child achievement: The direct role of parental expectations and the home environment. *Journal of Family Psychology,* 19(2), 294-304.

Epstein, J.L. (1996). *Perspectives and previews on research and policy for school, family, and community partnerships.* In A. Booth & J.F. Dunn (Eds.), Family-school links. Manwah, NJ.

Epstein, J. (2001). *School, family and community partnerships: Preparing educators and improving schools.* Boulder, CO: Westview Press.

Fan, X. & Chen X. (2001). Parental Involvement and Students' Academic Achievement: A Growth Modeling Analysis. *The Journal of Experimental Education,* 27-61.

Farid, M. & McMahan, D. (2004) *Accommodating and educating Somali students in Minnesota schools.* Saint Paul, Minnesota. Hamline University.

Fishbein, M., Triandis, H.C., Kanfer, F. H., Becker, M., Middlestadt, S.E., & Eichler, A. (2001). Factors influencing behavior and behavior change. In A. Baum, T.A. Revenson & J.E. Singer (Eds.), *Handbook of health psychologist* (pp. 3-17). Mahwah, NJ: Lawrence Erlbaum.

Floyd, L. (1998, March). *Joining hands: A parental involvement program.* Urban Education, 33, 1, 123-135.Lareau, A. (2000). Home advantage (2nd Ed.). Lanham, MD: Rowman & Littlefield Publishers, Inc.

García, E. E. (1994). *Understanding and meeting the challenge of student cultural diversity.* Boston: Houghton Mifflin.

Grolnick, W. S., Benjet, C., Kurowski, C. O., & Apostoleris, N. H. (1997). Predictors of parent involvement in children's schooling. *Journal of Educational Psychology, 89*(3), 538

Haager, D. (2007). Promises and cautions regarding using response to intervention with English language learners. *Learning Disability Quarterly, 30*(3), 213-218.

Hosp, J. & Reschly, D. J. (2004). Disproportionate representation of minority students in special education: academic, demographic, and economic predictors. *Exceptional Children, 70*(2), 185-199.

Huisman, K., Hough, M., Langellier, K., & Toner, C. (2011). *Somalis in Maine: Crossing cultural currents.* Berkeley, Calif.: North Atlantic Books.

Ihotu, A. (2011) .Staying off the bottom of the melting pot: Somali Refugees respond to a changing U.S. immigration Climate. *Bildhaan: An International Journal of Somali Studies*: Vol. 9, Article 11.

Kim, Y. Y., & Gudykunst, W. B. (1988). *Cross-cultural adaptation: Current approaches.* Sage Publications, Inc.

Ladson-Billings, G. (2006). From the achievement gap to the education debt: Understanding achievement in US schools. *Educational researcher, 35*(7), 3-12.

Lester, G., & Kelman, M. (1997). State disparities in the diagnosis and placement of pupils with learning disabilities, *Journal of Learning Disabilities,* 30(6), 559-607.

Lipsky, M. (1980). *Dilemmas of the individual in the public services.* Russell Sage Foundation. New York.

Machado-Casas, M. (2006). Narrating education of new indigenous/Latino transnational communities in the south: Migration, life, and its effects on schooling. (Doctoral dissertation, University of North Carolina at Chapel Hill). Dissertation Abstracts International (UMI No. 3207362).

Moll, L. C. & González, N. (2004) Engaging Life: A Funds of Knowledge Approach to Multicultural Education. In J. Banks & C. McGee Banks (Eds.), Handbook of research on multicultural education (pp. 699-715), San Francisco: Jossey-Bass.

No Child Left Behind.
https://nces.ed.gov/programs/coe/pdf/Indicator_CGF/
coe_cgf_2014_05.pdf No Child Left Behind Act.
2001. U.S.C. & PL107-110

Ogbu, J. U. (1978). *Minority education and caste: the
American system in cross-cultural perspective.* New
York: Academic Press.

Orfield, G., Losen, D., Wald, J., & Swanson, C. B. (2004).
Losing our future: How minority youth are being left
behind by the graduation rate crisis. *Civil Rights
Project at Harvard University (The).*

Park, J. (2007). Identifying children with disabilities in
ECLS-K. Paper presented at the Early Childhood
Longitudinal Study, Kindergarten Cohort Data Users'
Training, Washington, DC.

Pena, D. C. (2000). Parent involvement: Influencing factors
and implications. *The Journal of Educational
Research, 94*(1), 42-54.

Peterson, D . (1999). Parental involvement in the e
educational process. Eugene, OR ERIC
Clearinghouse On educational Management.

Portland Public Schools. portlandschools.org

Schumacher, S. (2009). *Research in education: Evidence-based inquiry.* (7th ed.). Boston, MA: Pearson

Scribner, A.P. (1999). High performing Hispanic schools: An
introduction. In P. Reyes, J.D. Scribner & A.P.
Scribner (Eds.), Lessons from high-performing
Hispanic schools: Creating learning communities.
New York: Teachers College Press.

Seidman, I. (2006). *Interviewing as qualitative research: A
guide for researchers in education and the social
sciences* (3rd ed.). New York: Teachers College
Press.

Senge, P., Camborn-McCabe, N. Lucas, T., Smith, B.,
Dutton, J. And Kleiner, A. (2000). Schools That
Learn. A Fifth Discipline Fieldbook for Educators,
Parents, and Everyone Who Cares About Education,
New York: Doubleday/Currency

Sosa, A.S. (1997). Involving Hispanic parents in educational
activities through collaborative relationships.
Bilingual Research Journal, 21, 2, 1-8.

Souto-Manning, M. (2006). A critical look at bilingualism
discourse in public schools: Autoethnographic
reflections of a vulnerable observer. *Bilingual
Research Journal*, 30, 559–577.

Stake, R. E. (1995). *The art of case study research.* Sage.

UN General Assembly Resolution 1386 (XIV) of 10
December 1959.
http://www.un.org/cyberschoolbus/humanrights/resou
rces/child.asp

United Nations Educational Scientific and Cultural
Organization (1985).
http://www.uis.unesco.org/Education/Documents/liter
acy-statistics-trends-1985-2015.pdf

United Nations High Commissioner for Refugees (2014)
http://www.unhcr.org/cgi-bin/texis/vtx/home

Urban, WJ, & Wagoner, JL (2003). American education: A
history. New York: McGraw- Hill. Washington, BT
(1995).

U.S. Population Survey. U.S. Census Bureau (2010).
http://www.census.gov/newsroom/releases/archives/p
opulation/cb11-tps16.html

Weber, M. (1910). *The theory of social and economic
organization.* New York: Talcott parsons

Wei, L. (2000). *The bilingual reader.* (1st ed). New York,
NY: Routledge.

Zentella, A.C. (2002). Latino® languages and identities. In M. Suarez-Orozco & M. Paez (Eds.). *Latinos: Remaking America* (pp. 321-338). Berkeley: University of California Press.

Concluding Thoughts

My past experience and present status influenced my decision to conduct this research. Conducting research on Somali parents' parental involvement in their children's schools, contributing to the existing knowledge about Somali people, and raising awareness about their conditions makes me feel as if I am giving back to my people, the Somali community.

I was born in one of the poorest districts of Mogadishu, Somalia. I started primary school at the age of six. In second grade, I was able to read and write in Somali. At grade five, I was transferred to an Arabic school. During my intermediate and secondary schooling, I learned Arabic and English. After the civil war broke out in 1990, I immigrated to Pakistan. I stayed in Pakistan close to ten years. During my stay there, I attended a post-secondary engineering school. In May, 2000 I was resettled in the United States as a refugee. As you see, my background and experiences are similar to the experiences of this study's participants: They came from the same region I came from; they were from poor families and at some point in their lives, they were refugees. Currently, we live in the same region sharing many characteristics as language minorities, Somalis, former refugees, parents, and Muslims.

As a native of Somalia and an educator in the Portland Public Schools, I witness the challenges and difficult circumstances that my people, Somalis in the Diaspora in general, and in Portland, Maine in particular, face. As an insider, I see the barriers the Somali community members face daily including schooling infused with Western conceptions of parenting, child development, and normality. Historically, ignorance and denial of diversity and its role in education increased these barriers. Like many Somalis, I am concerned that the schooling experiences in my new country do not satisfy my people's (Somalis') hope: to prepare their children for securing social and economic gains in order to break the cycle of poverty.

With my past and present in mind, I started to look at many different aspects of the educational system in the United States, including school and parent relationships, immigrant parents' involvement in, perceptions about, and understanding of U.S public education, and other language minority related aspects of public education. I see hardworking teachers who are frustrated by the below grade-level academic achievement and behavioral issues of some Somali students. I interact with parents (like Dowlo, Rahma,

226

Idil, Jama, and Farah) who have high expectations for their children yet are seen as uninvolved in their children's education. Power differences and conflict between parents and educators are observable in the community. However, I believe these conflicts and tensions can be used to strengthen parent-school relations if addressed with honest discussions and measured approaches (Christensen & Sheridan, 2001).

As I conclude the writing of my dissertation, I hope this work will be the beginning of my academic journey in the fields of language minority students and parental involvement.

SOMALI PARENT INVOLVEMENT IN THE

EDUCATION OF THEIR CHILDREN IN

AMERICAN MIDDLE SCHOOLS:

A CASE STUDY IN PORTLAND, MAINE

By

Abdullahi Ahmed

B.S. University of Engineering and Technology Peshawar,

1999

M.S.Ed. University of Southern Maine, 2005

A DISSERTATION

Submitted in Partial Fulfillment of the

Requirement for the Degree of

Doctor of Education

(in Educational Leadership)

The Graduate School

The University of Maine

December 2015

Advisory Committee:

Sarah Mackenzie, Associate Professor of

Educational Leadership, Advisor

Gordon Donaldson, Professor of Educational
Leadership, Emeritus

Flynn Ross, Associate Professor of Teacher
Education, University of Southern Maine

Julie Canniff, Associate Professor of Teacher
Education, Emerita University of Southern Maine

John Maddaus, Associate Professor of Curriculum
and Foundations

Made in the USA
Lexington, KY
15 November 2017